**Collins**

# CAPE® REVISION GUIDE

# MANAGEMENT OF BUSINESS

T0340513

**Kathleen Singh**

# Collins

HarperCollins Publishers Ltd
The News Building
1 London Bridge Street
London SE1 9GF

First edition 2015

10 9 8 7 6 5 4 3 2 1

© HarperCollins Publishers Limited 2015

ISBN 978-0-00-811606-4

www.collins.co.uk/caribbeanschools

A catalogue record for this book is available from the British Library

Typeset by QBS
Printed in Italy by Grafica Veneta S.p.A.

Author: Kathleen Singh
Illustrators: QBS
Publisher: Elaine Higgleton
Commissioning Editor: Tom Hardy
Managing Editor: Sarah Thomas
Copy Editor: Sylvia Worth
Proofreader: Carol Osborne

**Photo credits**
The publisher would like to thank the following for their kind permission to reproduce their photographs:

Page 9, J Ierich/Shutterstock; Page 29, Monkey Business Images/Shutterstock; Page 67, Blackred/Getty Images; Page 89, Aleksandr Kurganov/Shutterstock; Page 91, Robert Przybysz/Shutterstock; Page 91, ASA studio/Shutterstock; Page 92, Goran Bogicevic/Shutterstock; Page 125, Art Directors & TRIP/Alamy; Page 157, MJ Photography/Alamy

**Acknowledgements**
Special thanks for their contributions to this book to:
1. Mr. Curtis Bradley Nicholas Ramkissoon, BSc (UWI)
2. Miss Chantal Trishana Lutchman
3. Mr. Wendell Mahaste Singh

**Dedication**
This book is dedicated to all students in pursuit of excellence in the Management of Business.
Good luck and best wishes,

*Mrs. Kathleen Singh*

# Contents

# Guidelines for revision

## Your revision strategy

Everyone revises differently. You must use the methods that works best for you. But whatever methods you use, stick to them and be committed. The following suggestions may be helpful:

> **Plan ahead: This is most important. Make your plan and work to your plan.**
> **If you find parts of your course content are challenging, try to master these sections first.**
> **Work in groups with your classmates.**
> **Get help from your teachers.**
> **Use your own revision notes as a guide.**
> **Convert the information in your texts into real-life situations; use examples you are familiar with.**
> **Use past examination papers: these will help you to understand the structure of the examination questions.**
> **Make sure you understand the Key Concepts that are used in each module. These are listed below.**
> **When you have finished studying a topic, make notes. Grade yourself on your knowledge and understanding. Make any necessary comments on where further work might be helpful.**
> **You must attend all Revision classes that your teacher schedules. Remember that 'A teacher is worth more than a million books' (Chinese proverb).**
> **Study smart: It will guarantee great results.**

**Remember:** Your attitude determines your altitude!

## Key examination words

These words are used regularly in examination questions. It is important that you understand what they mean, so that you answer the questions in the correct way.

| Word | Meaning |
|---|---|
| Analyse: | give full details and an in-depth argument |
| Assess/Discuss: | present arguments for and against |
| Comment: | give an explanation, briefly |
| Define: | give the exact meaning of the term |
| Describe: | give a detailed account |
| Evaluate: | come to a conclusion and give reasons |
| Explain how: | give a clear account |
| Explain why: | give detailed reasoning |
| Justify: | give in-depth reasoning to support the view |
| Outline: | give an account |
| Recommend: | make a recommendation based on your argument |
| State: | give various points |

**Note:** If the question is based on calculations:

1. **State the formula you plan to use.**
2. **Use information from the question to put data into the formula.**
3. **Then do the calculations.**
4. **Then interpret the outcome of the calculations.**

# In the Examination Room

Try to remember the following points in the Examination Room.

1. Have a positive attitude. Relax. Keep calm. Believe in yourself. You have done a lot of work on this subject: now is your opportunity to show how much you have learned.
2. Read ALL instructions carefully. Select the questions that you can answer best.
3. Underline key words in the questions. Be sure you know *exactly* what the question is asking.
4. Make a plan for answering each question.
5. In answering the questions, make sure that each paragraph relates directly to the question asked.
6. Use examples to explain the points made. Examples will relate to the stimulus material given in the question. If none is provided, use examples from your own knowledge.
7. If for some reason the information for a particular question cannot be recalled, leave that question for the time being. Move on to the next question. Do not waste time. The information will very likely come back to you. Remain calm and confident.
8. Manage your time wisely. Allocate equal amounts for each question.
9. You **must** complete the required number of questions to guarantee the grade that you have been working to achieve.
10. Towards the end of the examination period, review your entire answer booklet:
    a. Be sure you have numbered the responses in your answer booklet as they are numbered in the question paper,
    b. Be sure that all response sheets are secured.

# Key concepts in business management

The following lists are of the key concepts in business management. Each one is explained in the following chapters. Use these as a checklist to ensure that you understand each of the key concepts.

## Unit 1 Module 1: Business and its environment

1. Articles of association
2. Charities
3. Consumer behaviour: choices, quality, responsibility
4. Continuity
5. Cooperative enterprise
6. Corporate culture
7. Decision-making
8. Ecological factors
9. Franchise
10. Globalisation
11. Growth
12. Holding companies
13. Human constraints
14. Incorporated & unincorporated
15. Joint venture
16. Legal personality
17. Limited liability
18. Macro environment
19. Market economy
20. Market share
21. Maximising profit
22. Memorandum of association
23. Mergers
24. Microenvironment
25. Mission statement
26. Mixed economy
27. Multinational
28. Nationalisation
29. Natural constraints
30. Non-governmental organisation
31. Operational objectives
32. Opportunity cost
33. Partnership
34. Planned economy
35. Primary sector
36. Private limited company
37. Private sector
38. Privatisation
39. Public limited company
40. Public sector
41. Secondary sector
42. Social ethics & environmental considerations
43. Sole trader
44. Statutory board
45. Social responsibility
46. Strategic objectives
47. Tactical objectives
48. Tariff
49. Tertiary sector
50. Trade liberalisation

## Unit 1 Module 2: Management of people

1. Abraham Maslow's hierarchy of needs
2. Accountability
3. Authority
4. Autocratic
5. Barriers to effective communication
6. Centralisation
7. Chain of command
8. Change: resistance & nature
9. Classical model
10. Coercive power
11. Communication
12. Communication networks
13. Communication channels & methods
14. Communication process
15. Compensation
16. Conflict
17. Contingency approach
18. Controlling
19. Critical thinking
20. Cultural bias
21. Decentralisation
22. Delegation
23. Democratic
24. Douglas McGregor: theory X & theory Y
25. Financial & non-financial
26. Formal & informal channels of communication
27. Frederick Taylor: Scientific Management Theory
28. Herzberg: Two Factor Theory
29. Group cohesiveness
30. Hierarchy
31. Human relations model
32. Human resource management
33. Industrial relations
34. Informal leadership
35. Job enlargement
36. Job enrichment
37. Job rotation
38. Laissez-faire
39. Leadership
40. Leading
41. Line & staff relationship
42. Lines of communication
43. Management by objectives
44. Management style
45. Management of change
46. Management of conflict
47. Off-the-job training
48. On-the-job training

49. Organisational culture
50. Organisational structure
51. Organising
52. Performance management
53. Piece rate
54. Quality circles
55. Planning
56. Rational economic man
57. Recruitment
58. Responsibility
59. Scarce resources
60. Selection
61. Selective perception
62. Self-actualisation
63. Span of control
64. Staffing
65. Systems approach
66. Teams/groups
67. Time rate
68. Trait theory
69. Transformational leadership style
70. Training & development
71. Participative leadership style
72. Work study

## Unit 1 Module 3: Business finance and accounting

1. Accounting information
2. Average rate of return
3. Balance sheet
4. Bonds
5. Book value
6. Break even
7. Budgetary control
8. Budgets
9. Capital
10. Capital markets
11. Cash flow statement
12. Current assets
13. Current liabilities
14. Debentures
15. Debt
16. Efficiency ratios
17. Equity
18. Feasibility study
19. Finance
20. Fixed liabilities
21. Gearing ratios
22. Gross profit margin
23. Income statement
24. International financial institutions
25. Investment appraisal
26. Investment capital
27. Investors ratios
28. Liquidity ratios
29. Long-term financing
30. Net present value
31. Net profit
32. Net profit margin
33. Margin of safety
34. Payback period
35. Regional financial institutions
36. Residual value
37. Shares
38. Short-term financing
39. Stock exchange
40. Variance
41. Venture capital
42. Working capital

## Unit 2 Module 1: Production and operations management

1. Absorption costing
2. Batch production
3. Benchmarking
4. Buffer stock
5. Capacity utilisation
6. Capital intensive
7. Cell production
8. Cellular layout
9. Consumer surveys
10. Contribution costing
11. Critical path analysis
12. Decision tree
13. Delphi technique
14. Design capacity
15. Direct cost
16. Diseconomies of scale
17. Dummy activity
18. Earliest start time (EST)
19. Economic order quantity (EOQ)
20. Economies of scale
21. Efficiency capacity
22. Fixed cost
23. Fixed position layout
24. Flow production
25. Forecasting
26. Integration
27. Jidoka
28. Job production
29. Jury of experts
30. Just-in-time (JIT)
31. Kaizen
32. Kanban
33. Labour intensive
34. Labour productivity
35. Latest finish time (LFT)
36. Lead time
37. Lean production
38. Machine productivity
39. Margin of safety
40. Method study
41. Miniaturisation
42. Modularisation
43. Moving averages
44. Opportunity cost
45. Outsourcing
46. Planning
47. Process layout
48. Product design brief

49. Production layout
50. Quality
51. Quality control
52. Quality assurance
53. Quality circles
54. Re-order level
55. Sales force composite
56. Specialisation
57. Standardisation
58. Stock turnover
59. Total float
60. Total quality management (TQM)
61. Types of stock
62. Value added
63. Value analysis
64. Work study

## Unit 2 Module 2: Fundamentals of marketing

1. Advertising
2. Behavioural segmentation
3. Boston Matrix
4. Brand loyalty
5. Channel of distribution
6. Cost plus pricing
7. Cultural factors
8. Demographic factors
9. Demographic segmentation
10. Economic factors
11. Focus groups
12. Geographic segmentation
13. Globalisation
14. Income elasticity of demand
15. Loss leader pricing
16. Macro environment
17. Marketing
18. Market intermediaries
19. Marketing mix
20. Marketing orientation
21. Market research
22. Markets
23. Market segmentation
24. Microenvironment
25. Niche marketing
26. Non-probability sampling
27. Penetration pricing
28. Pricing policies
29. Price elasticity of demand
30. Primary data
31. Probability sampling
32. Product development
33. Product extension
34. Production concepts
35. Production orientation
36. Product life cycle (PLC)
37. Product line
38. Retailer
39. Sales promotion
40. Secondary data
41. Segmentation
42. Selling concepts
43. Skimming pricing
44. Societal marketing
45. Surveys
46. Target marketing
47. Value added
48. Wholesaler
49. Zero level channel

## Unit 2 Module 3: Small business management

1. Break-even analysis
2. Business plan
3. Capital structure
4. Cash flows
5. Channel of distribution
6. Competitor analysis
7. Copyright
8. Corporate entrepreneurship
9. Direct mail
10. Distribution strategy
11. E-commerce
12. Economies of scale
13. Entrepreneur
14. Executive summary
15. External financing
16. Fixed economy
17. Globalisation
18. Government regulations
19. Human relations skills
20. Intellectual property
21. Internal financing
22. Location of business
23. Macro environment
24. Market research
25. Microenvironment
26. Market share
27. Mixed economy
28. One level channel of distribution
29. Partnership
30. Patent
31. Planned economy
32. Profit & loss
33. Promotion strategy
34. Social entrepreneurship
35. Sole trader
36. Target market
37. Trade liberalisation
38. Website
39. Word-of-mouth
40. Working capital

# Unit 1
## Module 1

## Business and its environment

# Types of economic activity

## Objectives

At the end of this section you will be able to:

1. Define the primary sector, secondary sector and tertiary sector of an economy
2. Distinguish between the various economic sectors of the economy.

## Introduction

Economic activity can be classified as primary, secondary and tertiary.

In underdeveloped economies their economic activity is essentially primary production.

In developing economies primary production is still a large part of the economic activity. However, the secondary level of production begins to develop. The tertiary level is very small.

In developed economies all sectors are developed, especially the tertiary sector. There exist therefore backward and forward linkages between economic growth and development.

### The primary sector

The primary sector is that part of the economy that is involved in the production of raw materials or the extraction of raw materials from the land. The primary sector includes agriculture, fishing, forestry, mining and quarrying. It is an important sector contributing to the economic gross national product.

**Gross national product (GNP):** this is the value of output produced within a country plus net property income from abroad. Gross domestic product plus net income from abroad equals gross national product.

### The secondary sector

This sector includes all firms that convert raw materials into finished goods. In developing economies, this sector grows faster than the primary sector. It contributes to increasing employment, improvement in the balance of payment and an improvement in people's standard of living.

### The tertiary sector

The tertiary sector is that part of the economy where the firms provide services to consumers and businesses.

Examples include banking, transport, insurance, tourism.

An increase in the size of this sector is evident as an economy develops.

---

## QUICK TEST

1. Define the following:
   a. Primary sector                                                     [5 marks]
   b. Secondary sector                                                   [5 marks]
   c. Tertiary sector                                                    [5 marks]
2. **Account for the size of various primary sectors in undeveloped and developing economies.**                                                    [15 marks]

# Economic sectors and legal structures

## Objectives

At the end of this section you will know:

1. Organisations that exist in the private and public sectors
2. The advantages and disadvantages of each organisation
3. The legal structure of each organisation
4. How they raise finance.

## Legal structure of the firm

There are two broad categories of business:

1. Incorporated
2. Unincorporated

### Incorporated business

> An incorporated business has a legal identity that is separate from the individual owners.
> The private sector includes: private limited companies (Ltd.), public limited companies (PLCs), cooperatives and friendly societies.
> These firms can own assets, owe money, and enter into contracts in their own right as they are recognised legally as a separate entity.
> They have limited liability.

### Unincorporated business

> In an unincorporated business, there is no distinction in the law between the owners and the business itself.
> These businesses include sole traders and partnerships.
> Liability is unlimited.

### Private sector organisations
### Sole trader

The features of a sole trader are:

> A sole trader is a one-man business.
> Owner provides all the capital.
> Owner provides all the labour.
> Unlimited liabilities.
> Owner undertakes all the risks.
> Owner enjoys all the profits.
> Owner makes all the decisions.
> Owner suffers all the losses.

The advantages and disadvantages of a sole trader are set out below.

| Advantages and disadvantages of sole trader ||
| Advantages | Disadvantages |
| --- | --- |
| > Easy to form | > Limited capital |
| > There is a closer relationship with customers | > Expansion is restricted because of lack of capital |
| > Owner can react immediately to customers' needs | > Does not benefit from economies of scale |
| > Owner is flexible; decision-making is quick | > Legal requirements, e.g. completing VAT records puts additional strain on owner |
| > Owner is motivated to work hard, as he is working for himself | > Owner cannot easily take a holiday |
| > Profits are not shared | > When owner dies the business usually dies with him |
| > Unlimited liability means owner is careful in making decisions | > Unlimited liability; if owner cannot pay debt he may lose personal assets as well as the business |
| > Secrecy is maintained | |
| > Can compete with larger firms because they are located in rural areas, where larger firms will not locate | |

## Partnership

Features of a partnership include:

> - **A partnership is a legal agreement.**
> - **Consists of two or more individuals.**
> - **Not a separate legal unit.**
> - **A Deed of Partnership may be drawn up, but it is not a legal requirement.**

Partnerships are common among professionals, for example lawyers.

The advantages and disadvantages of a partnership are set out below.

| Advantages and disadvantages of partnership | |
|---|---|
| **Advantages** | **Disadvantages** |
| › Simple to establish, i.e. not much legal procedure | › Personal unlimited liability |
| › Each partner contributes capital; more than a sole trader | › Decision-making can be slower because of the number of partners |
| › Greater economies of scale can be achieved | › A decision made by one partner is binding on the rest of the partners |
| › New ideas, as there are more partners | › Disagreement among partners |
| › There is specialisation, i.e. partners can specialise in a given area | › Insufficient capital; this hinders growth and expansion |
| › There are shared responsibilities | |
| › Decision-making can be more effective | › Profits are shared among partners |
| › Less personal stress than the sole trader | |
| › Continuity: if a partner dies their share of the business can be purchased by other partners | |
| › Easy to expand | |

## Private limited company

Features of a private limited company include:

> - **It consists of two to fifty shareholders.**
> - **It is governed by:**
>   - ○ **Memorandum of Association, which governs the external relationship of the company.**
>   - ○ **The Articles of Association, which governs the internal affairs of the business.**
> - **It enjoys limited liabilities.**
> - **The letters 'Co. Ltd.' must be included after the company's name.**

The advantages and disadvantages of a private limited company are set out below

| Advantages and disadvantages of private limited company | |
|---|---|
| **Advantages** | **Disadvantages** |
| › Shareholders have limited liability | › Legal formalities are involved in setting up the firm |
| › If a shareholder dies the business continues | › Capital is limited as shares cannot be sold on the open market |
| › It is a separate legal personality | › Shares are not easily transferable |
| › It can raise more capital from the sale of shares to employees, friends, family | › Limited contact with employees |
| › Economies of scale | |
| › Division of labour | |
| › Risks are spread among shareholders | |

## Public limited company

Features of a public limited company include:

> - **Stocks are sold to the public on the Stock Exchange.**
> - **The letters PLC must be included after the company's name.**
> - **Shares are transferable.**

*Don't forget!*

Limited liability: this is a concept that states shareholders of a firm are financially responsible for the amount of money they have invested in the firm. It means that should the firm become insolvent, shareholders will lose only the funds they have invested in the firm and not their personal assets.

The advantages and disadvantages of a public limited company are set out below.

| Advantages and disadvantages of public limited company | |
| --- | --- |
| Advantages | Disadvantages |
| › It is a separate legal entity | › Legal formalities are required in setting up the firm. High cost to the firm |
| › Limited liability for business debts | › Legal requirements: information must be disclosed to shareholders and the public |
| › Continuity | › Over-expansion can lead to diseconomies of scale |
| › Shares can be easily bought and sold | › There is the possible risk of a takeover as shares are sold on the open market |
| › Has access to more capital as shares can be sold on the open market | › The objectives of managers may be different from shareholders |
| › Enjoys the benefits of economies of scale | |
| › Risks are spread over many shareholders | |

## Cooperative enterprise

Features of a cooperative enterprise include:

› **All members contribute to the running of the business, e.g. share workload, responsibilities, and decision-making.**
› **All members have one vote.**
› **Profits are shared equally among members.**
› **Limited liabilities.**

The advantages and disadvantages of a cooperative enterprise are set out below.

| Advantages and disadvantages of cooperative enterprise | |
| --- | --- |
| Advantages | Disadvantages |
| › It is democratically merged | › There is a lack of business experience |
| › There is no conflict of interest | › Lack of capital as shares cannot be sold on the open market |
| › High level of motivation among members | › Slow decision-making |
| › Gain benefits from buying in bulk | › It is owned and managed by its members, who may not have the necessary skills and training. They may be less efficient and therefore face competition from larger firms |

## Franchise

Features of a franchise include:

› **It is not strictly a legal structure.**
› **It is a legal contract between two firms.**

The advantages of a franchise to the franchisor and franchisee are set out below.

| Advantages of a franchise | |
| --- | --- |
| Advantages to the franchisor | Advantages to the franchisee |
| › It reduces their cost of operation | › They can start a business that is already established |
| › It increases their market share | › Their advertising cost is reduced |
| › The established standards are maintained | › Training for staff borne by parent company |
| › It increases their cash flow; payment for the 'rights' and royalties as the firm operates | |

The disadvantages of a franchise to the franchisor and franchisee are set out below.

| Disadvantages to the franchisor | Disadvantages to the franchisee |
| --- | --- |
| › Their reputation will be affected if standards are not maintained | › Must buy inputs from franchisor |
| › Might receive lower royalty fees if franchisee does not declare accurate sales level | › Must pay royalties fees |
| › They can lose some trade secrets if franchisee breaks the agreement | › Cannot use their entrepreneurial skills |
| | › Must abide by the terms and conditions of the contract |

## Joint ventures

Features of a joint venture include:

› **A joint venture comprises two distinct firms that come together to share operations.**
› **Occurs where government partners with a local firm, or a foreign firm partners with a local firm.**
› **Control may be based on which firm has greater share of capital.**

The advantages and disadvantages of joint ventures are set out below.

| Advantages and disadvantages of joint ventures | |
| --- | --- |
| Advantages | Disadvantages |
| › Government can maintain control by owning the majority of the shares | › Firms can lose their trade secrets as they join with other firms |
| › Government will have the resources to employ improved technology | › Profits can be repatriated if one firm is based in a foreign country |
| › Decisions made will be beneficial to the country as a whole | |
| › It gives forging firms an opportunity to enter the domestic market | |

## Public sector organisations

These include:

**(a) Public Corporations**
**(b) Statutory Boards**

## Public corporations

Features of public corporations include:

› **Public corporations are owned by the state.**
› **They are public sector organisations.**
› **Their objective is to provide goods and services to the society at the lowest possible cost.**
› **Profit maximisation may not be an objective.**
› **They are involved in providing social services.**
› **They have a separate legal existence.**

The advantages and disadvantages of public corporations are set out below.

| Advantages and disadvantages of public corporations | |
| --- | --- |
| Advantages | Disadvantages |
| › They are financed by the government | › They might be inefficient |
| › Loss-making firms may still be kept functional if the benefit to society is greater than cost of production | › There is little incentive to be efficient as the state provides the funding |
| › Prices tend to be low | › Members of the Board may be politically affiliated |
| › They provide services to the society that are not serviced by profit-maximising private firms | › There may be too much government interference |
| › Resources of the state are used for the economy as a whole | |

## Statutory boards

Features of statutory boards include:

1. **Statutory boards are controlled by the state.**
2. **They report directly to a senior minister in the government; for example the Agricultural Society of Trinidad and Tobago is the statutory board for the Ministry of Agriculture.**

## Not-for-profit organisations:

A charity is an example of a not-for-profit organisation.
Features of charities include:

1. **The objective of charities is to create an awareness of the plight of the disadvantaged in society.**
2. **They obtain funding from fund-raising events they organise and from donations.**
3. **They do not pay taxes.**
4. **Businesses can claim any donations to charities as a tax deduction.**

## Nationalisation
### Nationalised industry

Features of a nationalised industry:

1. **A nationalised industry is owned wholly or partly by the government.**
2. **Earns some of its revenue by selling its goods and services.**
3. **Controlled by a board of directors appointed by a government minister.**
4. **Answerable to the public for its activities.**
5. **Large firm in terms of sales, employment and capital employed.**
6. **Provides a vital service to the economy.**

The advantages and disadvantages of a nationalised industry are set out below.

| Advantages and disadvantages of nationalised industry | |
| --- | --- |
| **Advantages** | **Disadvantages** |
| › Socially important services: will not be supplied by the private sector because they are unprofitable | › Government interference: nationalised industries are always subject to government interference |
| › Natural monopolies: it may be efficient for one firm to provide the service and reap the benefits of economies of scale | › Inefficient: there is no need to be efficient as government will provide all the funding to cover losses |
| › Advanced technology: a firm in the private sector may be unwilling to risk large sums of money to purchase the technology | › Competition: there is no competition so little is done in terms of research and development |
| › Strategic goods and services: strategic industries must be controlled by the state to ensure supply of output in times of wars | › Objectives: there is conflict of objectives. What the government wants and the objectives of the firm may differ |
| › Unemployment: government may nationalise a firm if it is going bankrupt to ensure workers remain employed | |

## Privatisation

The advantages and disadvantages of privatisation are set out below.

| Advantages and disadvantages of privatisation | |
| --- | --- |
| **Advantages** | **Disadvantages** |
| › Competition: it leads to competition and greater efficiency | › Private monopolies: privatisation creates private monopolies, i.e. consumers are not protected |
| › Decision-making: is faster | › Social responsibilities: these are neglected in a privatised firm |
| › Motivation: it leads to a more motivated workforce | › 'Selling off the family silver': the revenue from the sale of previously owned state assets was too little |
| › Finance: the sale of state assets can provide revenue for the government | › Competition: privatisation has not created competition. It has led to consumers complaints about poor quality |
| › Control: government can set up regulation policies to guard against consumer exploitation | |

| | |
|---|---|
| › Taxpayer: taxpayers benefit as government will not have to finance nationalised industries | |
| › Trade union: their power is weakened | |
| › Government interference: there is little government interference. Firms can pursue their own objectives | |
| › It attracts foreign investment | |

## Problems in changing from one legal structure to another

### Changing from a sole trader to a partnership
Problems may include:

1. There is a legal document that governs it.
2. Loss of control as there are more partners.
3. Decision-making takes longer.
4. Any decision made by one partnership is bound by all partners; so if one partner makes a bad decision, all partners may lose.
5. Loss of flexibility so it cannot respond immediately to market demand.
6. Loss of personal contact with customers and partners.
7. Profits have to be shared among partners.

### Changing from a private limited company to a public limited company
Problems include:

1. Secrecy is lost.
2. Workers may feel left out of decision-making.
3. All accounts must be made public so people may buy shares.
4. Powerful shareholders may dominate the business.
5. There may be conflict of interest between managers and shareholders.
6. It can over-expand and this can lead to problems of coordination and control, leading to diseconomies of scale.

### Changing from a partnership to a private limited company
Problems include:

1. There may still be financial problems as shares can only be sold to people privately: capital cannot be raised by sale of shares.
2. Shares are not transferable.
3. They must have a legal structure, governed by the Memorandum of Association and Articles of Association.

---

QUICK TEST

1. State the advantages and disadvantages of the sole trader and partnership.  [10 marks]
2. What are the advantages of a franchise to
   a. The franchisor
   b. The franchisee  [10 marks]
3. Discuss the advantages of nationalisation and privatisation to the domestic economy.  [20 marks]

# Business objectives

## Objectives

At the end of this section you will know:

1. **What objectives are**
2. **The different type of objectives a firm will set**
3. **The importance of setting objectives**

### The nature of objectives

Objectives should:

> **Be acceptable to the workforce.**
> **Be achievable.**
> **Motivate staff.**
> **Be measurable.**
> **Be capable of being broken down into shorter periods of time.**
> **Be fairly rigid but allow for a small measure of flexibility, where necessary.**
> **Be in keeping with higher level objectives of the firm.**
> **Be simple enough to be understood by all workers in the firm.**
> **Be communicated to workers.**
> **Have worker input, where possible.**

### Importance of objectives

Objectives are important in:

> **Providing a guide for the operation of the firm.**
> **Providing a sense of direction and unity for the firm.**
> **Coordinating the firm's activity.**
> **Motivating employees.**
> **Measuring and controlling the activities of the firm.**
> **Providing the basis for decision-making.**
> **Giving shareholders an account of the business.**
> **Indicating the strengths of the firm, to point out weaknesses and allow action to be taken.**

### Objectives must be 'SMART'

That is, objectives must be:

> **Specific**
> **Measurable**
> **Attainable**
> **Realistic**
> **Timed.**

### Objectives of the various stakeholders

The objectives of various stakeholders are set out below.

| Objectives of various stakeholders | | | | |
|---|---|---|---|---|
| Shareholders | Employees | Customers | Suppliers | Government |
| › High dividends | › Job security | › High-quality goods | › Fair price for supplies | › Employment |
| › Growth of the business | › Fair wage | › Fair prices | › Prompt payment | › Efficient use of resources |
| › Healthy corporate image | › Good working condition | › Good service | › Continued demand for supplies | › Obey health & safety laws |
| | › Scope for promotion | › Innovation | | › Abide by consumer protection laws |

### Short-, medium- and long-term objectives

> **Short-term: operational objectives:**
>  o These are made by lower-level management.
>  o Example: to increase weekly sales from 1,000 units to 1,500 units.
> **Medium-term: tactical objectives:**
>  o These are made by middle management.
>  o Example: to improve efficiency/productivity by 10 per cent in 9 months' time.

> **Long-term: strategic objectives:**
>   o These are made by top management.
>   o Examples: to diversify the firm's output in 4 years; to enter into the overseas market in 5 years.

## Hierarchy of objectives
## Vision

> **This is necessary for the success of any business.**
> **It reflects the ideas and philosophies of all personnel involved in establishing the firm.**
> **It will include what the firm expects to achieve in the short-term, medium-term and long-term.**
> **From this vision the mission statement will be established and from the mission statement will follow the strategic, tactical and operational objectives.**

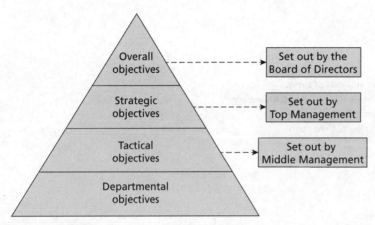

Hierarchy of objectives

## Mission statement
The features of the mission statement are as follows:

> **The mission statement sets out the purpose of the business.**
> **This must be communicated to and understood by all the employees and shareholders.**
> **Most mission statements refer to the values of the business and the main purpose.**
> **It is used to provide the framework for running the firm.**
> **It must constantly be revisited to ensure that the firm's operation is in keeping with the mission statement.**
> **It serves as a compass which guides the business.**
> **The strategic and tactical objectives flow from the mission statement.**

## Strategic objectives
The features of strategic objectives are as follows:

> **These are broad based objectives that state what the firm hopes to achieve in the long-run (e.g. the next 5 years).**
> **They tend to be more measurable.**
> **Strategic objectives may include the following:**
>   o Survival
>   o Increase sales by 10 per cent in the next 3 years
>   o Increase market share by 20 per cent in the next 5 years.

## Tactical objectives
The features of tactical objectives are as follows:

> **These are designed to ensure that the strategic objectives are met.**
> **They are more detailed and generally short-term.**
> **They relate to the individual departments within the firm.**
> **They are quantitative, that is, they can be measured mathematically.**

 QUICK TEST

1. **Explain the importance of objectives to a named firm.** [15 marks]
2. **Explain what tactical objectives are and give examples.** [5 marks]
3. **Explain what strategic objectives are and give examples.** [5 marks]
4. **Explain what operational objectives are and give examples.** [5 marks]

# Business ethics and corporate social responsibility

## Objectives

At the end of this section, you will know:

1. **The importance of business ethics**
2. **The social responsibilities of the firm.**

## Business ethics

Ethical behaviour is subjective. In broad terms, ethical behaviour is behaviour that is seen to be morally earned. The terms 'ethical' and 'legal' overlap; however, some unethical practices may not be illegal.

### An ethical code

This is a formal business document that states the rules that management should follow when faced with a decision. For example:

> **Should the firm relocate to a country paying a lower wage rate?**
> **Should the firm put on the market a life-saving drug after limited testing?**
> **Should advertising aimed at children be restrained?**

### Forms of social responsibilities and ethical practices

These include:

1. **Preserving the environment.**
2. **Obeying the laws of the land, paying taxes, obeying health and safety regulation.**
3. **Giving consumers value for money.**

### The importance of business ethics

Business ethics refer to the set of principles which guide business decisions.
They are important for the following reasons:

1. **They improve the image of the firm.**
2. **They can lead to an increased market share.**
3. **They can lead to increased sales.**
4. **The firm's profit margin will increase.**
5. **They will create a better society.**
6. **They are necessary for the survival of the firm.**
7. **Some unethical practices are punishable my law.**
8. **They attract staff.**

### Obligations to stakeholders

The firm has various obligations to its stakeholders. (Note: the distinction between stakeholders and shareholders.)

Don't forget!

Integrity: this implies the honesty with which a firm conducts its business activities. This honesty must be exhibited in the firm's relationship with its various stakeholders.

#### Employees

Obligations to employees include:

1. **Secure reasonably paid employment**
2. **Safe working conditions**
3. **Compensation for injuries sustained on the job**
4. **Proper training.**

#### Customers

Obligations to customers include:

1. **Good quality products**
2. **Competitive prices**
3. **To conduct market research to improve the product**
4. **To refrain from misleading advertising.**

#### Suppliers

Obligations to suppliers include:

1. **Fair prices**
2. **Regular customers**
3. **Prompt payment.**

## Owners

Obligations to owners include:

1. **High profit margin**
2. **Increase in share prices**
3. **Increase in dividends**
4. **Protecting the firm's assets**
5. **Providing the necessary accounting information.**

## Society

Obligations to society include:

1. **Avoid polluting the environment**
2. **Conserving resources**
3. **Creating employment**
4. **Preserving local culture and encouraging its expansion.**

## Government

Obligations to government include:

1. **Efficient use of resources**
2. **Pay taxes**
3. **To observe all regulations regarding trade, both domestic and international.**

 QUICK TEST

1. **Explain the following concepts:**
   a. Business ethics
   b. Ethical code        **[10 marks]**
2. **Discuss the obligations of a firm to its stakeholders.**        **[15 marks]**

# Decision-making

## Objectives

At the end of this section you will know:

1. The essential features of information for decision-making
2. The factors affecting decision-making
3. The process of decision-making

## Essential features of information for decision-making

It is essential that information required for decision-making is:

1. **Accurate:** information upon which a decision is based should be accurate.
2. **Timely:** the information must be as recent as possible.
3. **Relevant:** the data must be relevant to the given situation.
4. **Cost-effective:** the cost of collecting the data must be less than the benefits to be gained.

### Qualitative and quantitative decision-making

Quantitative data and qualitative data are complements to each other.

### Qualitative factors

The following are the qualitative factors that affect decision-making:

1. **The environment:** this must be considered when making location decisions.
2. **The labour supply:** the quality of labour supply is vital. This looks at factors such as skills, training and work ethics.
3. **Management skills and experience:** will be a major factor in a decision the firm takes.
4. **Laws:** any decision a firm makes must be subject to government regulations.

### Quantitative factors

The following are examples of quantitative data that affect decision-making:

1. **Sales**
2. **Profit**
3. **The labour supply:** the number of potential workers.

### Stages in decision-making

1. **Objectives:**
   a. Before making a decision, it is important to decide on the aims and objectives of the firm.
   b. Then proceed as follows.
2. **Definition of the problem:** e.g. fall in demand for the firm's output
3. **Data collection:**
   a. Primary data: questionnaires
   b. Secondary data: e.g. sales data from competitors.
4. **Analysis and evaluation of data:**
   a. What does primary data show
   b. What does secondary data show
   c. Evaluate each option.
5. **Formulate and test alternative strategies:**
   a. Select the best alternative
   b. Example: enter new markets; use advertising and sales promotions to sell more in existing markets.
6. **Implement the decision.**
7. **Implement the alternative selected.**
8. **This will need more finance and personnel.**
9. **Establish specific targets:** e.g. 10 per cent increase in sales in 18 months.
10. **Evaluation of decision:** did the firm achieve its original objectives? If it did not, then further management action will be needed.

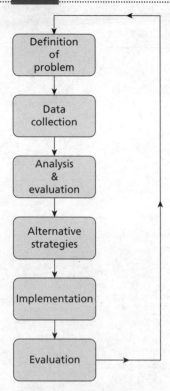

Illustration to show **stages** in decision-making

## Factors affecting decision-making

There are a number of factors both internal and external that a firm must consider when making any decision. These include the following:

1. **The government, political and legal factors:**
   a. The state encourages and guides the private sector
   b. Provides cash subsidies to firms
   c. Tax concessions
   d. Regulates and controls the private sector firms; e.g. minimum wage legislation, health and safety regulations
   e. Is a buyer of goods and services
   f. Laws.
2. **Social and cultural factors:**
   a. These determine the size of the market
   b. The supply of labour
   c. Demographic trends
   d. Life cycles, values, beliefs, working wives, one-person households.
3. **Technology will impact on business decisions in the following ways:**
   a. The demand for the firm's product: the market
   b. In the production process: cost of production
   c. The size of the workforce
   d. The way workers are managed
   e. The skill of the workforce
   f. The way the business communicates.
4. **Economic factors**
   **The following economic factors will affect business decisions:**
   a. Rate of inflation
   b. Exchange rate
   c. Balance of payments
   d. Level of employment in the economy
   e. Rate of interest
   f. Taxation policies
   g. Trade cycle
   h. Level of income in the economy.

5. **Ecological factors**
   **Any decision that a firm makes must include the preservation of the environment.**

6. **Human constraints**
   **Business decisions are limited by the following human factors:**
   a. Strength and power of trade unions
   b. Qualification and numbers of staff presently employed
   c. Ability of the staff to accept change
   d. Supply of labour in the market.

---

 QUICK TEST

1. **State the essential features of information for decision-making.**       **[8 marks]**
2. **Discuss the stages of decision-making in a named firm.**       **[15 marks]**
3. **Discuss the factors affecting decision-making in a named firm.**       **[15 marks]**

# Impact of globalisation on business

## Objectives

At the end of this section you will:

1. Know the advantages and disadvantages of multinationals to the host countries.
2. Be able to evaluate the impact of globalisation on Caribbean businesses.

## Multinational company

A multinational company (MNC) is one that has its headquarters in the metropolitan country and subsidiaries in developing countries.

### Growth and expansion of MNCs

> The reason for their growth and expansion has been the belief that vertically integrated companies would have a competitive advantage over local companies that do not have the finance or technology to compete in overseas markets.
> MNCs benefit from economies of scale. They have the experience in strategic planning, forecasting, market research, finance, production and marketing, and are able to have effective communication with subsidiaries.
> Government policy of 'Industrialisation by Invitation' had a huge impact on the development of MNCs.

Don't forget!

Vertically integrated: this situation occurs when two firms join together, but they are at different stages in the production process.

Backward vertical integration occurs where a firm buys out, or is connected to, the supplier of its raw materials. Forward integration occurs where the firm buys out its customer.

The advantages and disadvantages of MNCs to a host country are set out below.

| MNCs | |
| --- | --- |
| **Advantages to host country** | **Disadvantages to host country** |
| > Create employment: they create employment for skilled and unskilled labour | > Policy making takes place in metropolitan country, so the interest of the host country might not be considered |
| > Transfer of technology: they bring to the host country ideas and expertise, advanced techniques and skills | > Research and development facilities and programmes are carried out in the metropolitan country |
| > Modern work practices introduced: e.g. employee participation in some areas of decision-making | > They create enclaves in the economy: the technologically advanced sector and the traditional sector. The former have high wages, while the latter have low wages |
| > Tax revenue: this is a major form of revenue for the government of Trinidad & Tobago | > There is very little transfer of technology |
| > Earner of foreign exchange: this is important to pay for imports | > They repatriate their profits, therefore the multiplier effect does not take place in the host country |
| > Improves the balance of payments | > Because of their strength, they can hold third world economies to ransom |
| > Leads to the creation of other firms: these firms provide some of the input they need | > They aim to maximise profits: wherever they can change location to increase profit margins, they will do just that |
| > Social responsibilities:<br>  o Preserving the environment<br>  o Providing scholarships for locals<br>  o Financial support to the local culture, such as Carnival, Divali, Eid in Trinidad & Tobago<br>  o Funding for development, such as libraries, etc.<br>  o Providing employment programmes in rural areas, as well as schooling in such areas | > They deplete the non-renewable resources |
| | > They can pollute the environment |
| | > Poor working conditions |
| | > The policies of multinationals may not always benefit the host country |
| | > The multinational concentrates on own interest rather than that of the host country. They may decide at short notice to move production out of the country, resulting in unemployment, balance of payment problems and affecting economic growth |
| | > They can exploit cheap labour and raw materials with no regard for the environment. |

## The role of the government

Government's policy of 'Industrialisation by Invitation' offers attractive benefits to multinationals, such as, for example:

› **Tax holidays**
› **Cheap source of energy**
› **Adequate infrastructure**
› **Repatriation of profits.**

## Trade liberalisation and globalisation

Trade liberalisation involves freer international trade with fewer restrictions.
The benefits include:

› **Wider variety of goods.**
› **Domestic firms are forced to improve their quality to compete with foreign firms.**
› **Countries can now specialise, reaping the benefits of economies of scale.**
› **Links are created with other countries.**

## Impact on consumers

› **Consumers have access to wider variety of goods.**
› **Prices are lower because of competition in the market.**
› **Consumers have access to internet shopping.**
› **Consumers have access to better quality of goods.**

## Impact on Caribbean businesses

The positive and negative impacts of trade liberalisation and globalisation on Caribbean businesses are given below

| Positive and negative impacts of trade liberalisation and globalisation on Caribbean businesses | |
| --- | --- |
| Positive impacts: | Negative impacts: |
| › To enter overseas market | › Competition may force inefficient firms out of the market |
| › Create linkages with foreign firms | › May even lose market share in the domestic economy |
| › Domestic firms can grow and expand | › May not have the resources to purchase new technologies |
| › Foreign exchange | › May not have the human resources to use the new technologies |
| › Access to new technologies | › More money spent to advertise in order to maintain market share |
| › Economies of scale | › More money spent on market research to maintain market share |
| › Increase efficiency | |
| › Cheaper sources of raw materials | |
| › Learning by doing | |
| › Foreign investors will be attracted | |
| › Greater access to foreign capital | |
| › Screwdriver industries will locate in the domestic economy | |
| › Creation of linkages in the domestic economy | |

## Impact on the economy

› **Trade increases**
› **Increase in foreign exchange**
› **Unemployment may occur**
› **Smaller firms may not be able to compete or survive**

## Impact on the government

› **Multinationals can become too powerful; therefore, government may have to face MNCs as a possible pressure force.**
› **Government has to deal with increasing crime rate.**

Don't forget!

Screwdriver industry: an industry that is essentially footloose, that is; it can be located anywhere. It is essentially an assembly industry. It imports the components and then assembles the parts into the finished products; these industries are normally found in the developing countries.

QUICK TEST

1. Discuss the advantages of multinationals in a named economy.  [10 marks]
2. Discuss the disadvantages of multinationals in a named economy.  [10 marks]
3. Discuss the effects of trade liberalisation on Caribbean economies.  [15 marks]

## Essay questions

1. a. Define the following:
      i.   Strategic objectives
      ii.  Tactical objectives
      iii. Operational objectives  [6 marks]
   b. Discuss the importance of setting objectives to a named firm.  [14 marks]
   c. Why is it necessary for firms to revisit their objectives?  [5 marks]
   [Total = 25 marks]

2. a. Discuss the stages in decision-making.  [10 marks]
   b. Evaluate the factors affecting decision-making.  [15 marks]
   [Total = 25 marks]

3. Discuss the advantages and disadvantages of multinationals to the domestic economy.
   [25 marks]

## Key concepts

**Ethics:** are moral principles that should be at the base of decision-making.

**Franchise:** a business based upon the name, logo, and training methods of an existing successful business.

**Mission statement:** brief outline of the general purpose of a business. It aims to provide a sense of direction to all employees in the organisation.

**Nationalisation:** the process of transferring firms from the private sector to the public sector.

**Primary sector:** that part of the economy consisting of all extractive industries, agricultural, fishing, lumbering, etc.

**Privatisation:** the process of returning firms that were once owned by the government to the private sector.

**Secondary sector:** that part of the economy that is involved in manufacturing.

**Tertiary sector:** that part of the economy that deals with services.

# MULTIPLE CHOICE QUESTIONS

1. The provision of services will fall in which Level of Production?
   a. Subsistence
   b. Primary
   c. Tertiary
   d. Manufacturing

2. Firms become multinational for the main purpose of:
   a. Transferring Technology
   b. Providing Revenue for the host country
   c. Providing goods and services for the host country
   d. Reducing their overall cost of operation

3. The advantage large firms have over small firms is referred to as:
   a. Economies of scale
   b. Profit maximisation
   c. Profit sharing
   d. Retained profits

4. Which of the following are the criteria for measuring the size of a firm?
   I. Level of output
   II. Market share
   III. The number of workers employed
   IV. The level of competition in the market
   a. I, II
   b. II, III, IV
   c. I, II, III
   d. I, II, III, IV

5. Horizontal Integration can best be described as a situation where:
   a. Two firms merge that are in the same industry and at the same stage of production
   b. Firms come together
   c. Large firms take over smaller firms
   d. Workers of two firms integrate

6. Government payment to local producers in the form of a tax relief to reduce their cost of production is:
   a. Benefit
   b. Tariff
   c. Quota
   d. Subsidy

7. Cost push inflation is caused by:
   a. Lower cost of production
   b. An increase in the cost of its inputs
   c. An increase in the money supply
   d. An increase in the demand for the firms output

8. A firm is engaged in ethical behaviour when:
   a. Moral principles are an integral part of its decision-making
   b. Moral principles are not taken into account in its decision-making process
   c. It employs child labour
   d. When it pays managers high wages

9. Which of the following are the advantages of Nationalised Companies?
   I. Their objective is consumer welfare
   II. They are inefficient and wasteful
   III. They avoid duplication of scarce resources
   IV. They benefit from economies of scale
   a. I, III
   b. I, III, IV
   c. III, IV
   d. I, II, III, IV

10. The Memorandum of Association is a document that:
    I. Governs the external relationship of the firm
    II. Gives details of a company's purpose in trading
    III. The amount of capital it needs to raise
    IV. Gives the company's registered name and address
    a. I, III, IV
    b. II, III, IV
    c. I, II
    d. I, II, III, IV

11. Which of the following pieces of information would be found in the articles of association of a company?
    I. The rights of shareholders
    II. The powers of directors
    III. Rules governing formal company meetings
    IV. Borrowing powers of the company
    a. I, III, IV
    b. II, III, IV
    c. I, II, III, IV
    d. I, II

12. Which of the following are the benefits of Multinational Corporations to the host country?
    I. The repatriation of profits
    II. The creation of employment
    III. Increase in tax revenue for the government
    IV. An increase in Gross Domestic Product for the host country
    a. I, II
    b. II, III, IV
    c. I, IV
    d. I, II, III, IV

13. The following are the internal benefits of a firm as it increases in size:
    I. Technical economies
    II. Managerial economies
    III. Purchasing economies
    IV. Risk-bearing economies
    a. I, II
    b. I, III, IV
    c. II, III, IV
    d. I, II, III, IV

**14.** Which of the following is not an argument of privatisation?

a. It increases the efficiency of the firm

b. It improves the quality of the firm's output

c. It raises large sums of money for the government

d. It increases the level of employment

**15.** The advantages of a mixed economy is that:

I. The state provides public goods

II. The private sector provides goods and services to maximise profits

III. The state regulates the operations of private sector firms

IV. The state attempts to maximise profits

a. I, II, III

b. II, III, IV

c. I, II, III, IV

d. II, III

**16.** The advantages of line organisation are:

I. Unity of command

II. Clear chain of command

III. Clear line of communication

IV. Overloads key people

a. I, IV

b. I, II, III

c. III, IV

d. I, II, III, IV

**17.** The advantage of decentralisation is:

a. The views of domestic consumers are not considered

b. Some workers will lose their jobs

c. That decision making takes a longer time

d. It takes into account differences in the culture and consumer taste

**18.** The critical path analysis is used as a decision making tool when:

a. Important decisions have to be made

b. Scheduling and controlling large projects

c. The production department is not efficient

d. The project to be undertaken is costly

# Unit 1
## Module 2

# The management of people

# Functions and theories of management

## Objectives

At the end of this section, you will know:

1. **The contributions of the following management theories to firms today:**
   a. Classical model
   b. Human relations model
   c. Systems approach
   d. Contingency approach.
2. **The functions of management.**

## Evolution of management theories (principles and contribution to modern-day organisations)

### Classical model:

This includes the work of **F. W. Taylor, Henri Fayol and Max Weber.** The main feature of the classical theorists is that very little importance is attached to the value of the worker.

1. **F. W. Taylor's views are still applicable:**
   a. Money motivates
   b. Observe and recording staff performance
   c. Efficiency is a key note
   d. Workers are still paid by piece-rate system.
2. **Henri Fayol:**
   a. Established the functions of management.
   b. The span of control should be between three and six.
   c. There should be tight managerial control.
   d. There are physical and mental limitations to any single manager's ability to control people and activities.
   e. A narrow span of control has the advantage of a tight control and close supervision. It allows for better coordination of subordinates' activities.
   f. It gives managers time to think and plan.
   g. There is better communication with subordinates.
   h. Fayol's principles of management are still used today:
      i. Division of work
      ii. Authority
      iii. Discipline
      iv. Order
      v. Scalar chain
      vi. Centralisation
      vii. Pay
      viii. Individual interest takes second place to firm's interest
      ix. Unity of command
      x. Unity of direction
      xi. Equity
      xii. Stability for workers
      xiii. Initiative
      xiv. Esprit de corps.
3. **Max Weber (German sociologist):**
   His approach to management:
   a. Clearly defined hierarchy
   b. Division of labour
   c. Impersonal relationship
   d. Detailed rules and regulations
   e. Useful for large organisation, bureaucracy is necessary
   f. There is therefore accountability
   g. A hierarchy still exists in the firms today

### Human relations model (Elton Mayo)
1. **The human relations model recognises:**
   a. Employees as humans with special needs
   b. That social pressure from co-workers has a tremendous effect on workers' level of productivity
   c. Group standards determine the workers' level of output
   d. Group allegiance is more valuable than money
2. **Contribution to modern organisations:**
   a. The human relation model is applicable today; most firms have placed emphasis on workers' needs in decision-making
   b. It reinforces the value of the human resources department

### Systems approach
1. **The systems theory is based on the fact that any given firm consists of divisions or departments, each performing valuable functions.**
2. **When a systems approach is adopted, managers have to decide how a change in a department will affect other departments before making that change.**
3. **The systems approach to management regards firms as groups of inter-relating parts that require coordination and the necessary information, in order for the firm to convert inputs into finished outputs. It looks at the various functional areas in the firm; for example, the marketing department, the production department, the finance department, the human resource department. Each department is regarded as a subset of the entire firm. Each sub-system or department must perform its function efficiently in order to guarantee the proper and efficient functioning of the entire firm. It means, therefore, that before any management decision is made, the effects this decision will have on the other departments or subsection must be fully explored. It is a system most managers try to implement.**
4. **The concept of synergy is a principle upon which the systems theory is based. It means the whole is greater than the sum of its parts. It means that if one department of the firm is not performing efficiently, this could have a negative effect on the entire firm.**
5. **Contributions to modern organisation:**
   a. Used by organisations in decision-making
   b. Most organisations employ the wisdom of the systems theory

### The contingency approach
1. **The contingency approach is based on the fact that management decisions are based on the given situation**
2. **Management therefore will use a combination of different theories to deal with different issues; e.g. Taylor's classical model and Mayo's human relations model.**
3. **Contribution to modern organisations:**
   a. Different approaches can be used to find the right fit.
   b. It can be applied to an organisation undergoing change.

## Functions of management
1. **Planning: defining the aims and objectives of the firm.**
2. **Organising: allocating resources to achieve objectives.**
3. **Leading and directing:**
   a. Leading involves using influence to motivate workers to achieve established goals.
   b. Directing involves giving orders and instructions.
4. **Controlling: this involves ensuring the firm's objectives are being met. If not, to take corrective action.**
5. **Staffing: ensuring that the human resource is adequate and fully trained.**
6. **Coordinating the activities of the various departments.**

---

QUICK TEST
.................................................................................

1. **Discuss the importance of the following to businesses today:**
   a. F. W. Taylor                                                    **[10 marks]**
   b. Henri Fayol                                                     **[10 marks]**
   c. Max Weber                                                       **[10 marks]**
2. **Discuss the functions of management to a named firm.**           **[15 marks]**

# Organisational structure

## Objectives

At the end of this section, you will know the:

1. Classification of organisational structure.
2. Advantages and disadvantages of the structures.
3. Characteristics of a formal organisational structure.

## Classification of organisational structure (principles, advantage and disadvantages)

**Organisational structure may be classified in the following ways:**

1. **By function**
   a. Jobs are grouped together and organised into departments, sections or functions; e.g. marketing, finance, and production.
   b. It can lead to:
      i. Clearly defined channels of communication.
      ii. Clearly defined hierarchy.
      iii. Clearly defined roles.
      iv. Decision-making is more centralised.
   c. The advantage is that it allows for specialisation.
   d. The problems include:
      i. Communication is poor
      ii. The more levels of hierarchy, the higher is the cost.
      iii. It is flexible.
      iv. There are more levels of the hierarchy as the business grows.

2. **By product**
   a. Here the functional areas of the firm work together.
   b. The advantage is that it allows individuals to specialise.
   c. Decision-making is faster:
      i. Greater interdependence
      ii. Greater flexibility for growth
      iii. More profit activities can be added.
   d. The possible problems:
      i. There may be duplication of management in all decisions
      ii. Rivalry between decisions
      iii. There may be difficulty in coordinating a large number of divisions.

3. **By geographical market**
   a. Used by businesses which operate across international borders, e.g. multinationals.
   b. Each geographical area can organise staff into product or functional divisions.
   c. Each geographical area operates as a separate profit centre.
   d. Advantage is that each centre can cater to the specific needs of the local consumer.
   e. Potential problems:
      i. Each geographical area may become too dependent on the head office.
      ii. Each area may become too independent.
      iii. They may not adhere to ethical standards.

4. **By matrix**
   a. The objective here is to create flexibility into the structure of the organisation.
   b. It involves organising teams that cross normal departmental boundaries.
   c. This can result in:
      i. Experts from different functions coming together to work on a project promoting a wider viewpoint.
      ii. Decision-making is more centralised.
      iii. There is increased delegation.
      iv. Project managers are responsible for projects rather than functional heads.
      v. Confusion with employees having to report to two managers, i.e. functional head and project manager.

| Advantages and disadvantages of a matrix organisation structure | |
|---|---|
| **Advantages** | **Disadvantages** |
| › Communication is improved | › Teams may have more than one individual to report to |
| › Coordination between departments | › Project teams may develop |
| › Improved decision-making | › Loyalty to each other and not the organisation |
| › Can allow individuals to use particular skills within a variety of contexts | › There may not be a clear line of accountability for project teams |
| › Avoids the need for several departments to meet regularly, so reducing costs and improving coordination | |

5. **By team**
   a. A team is a group of people with a common aim.
   b. An effective team must possess the following characteristics: trust, commitment, participation, flexibility, decision by consensus, encouragement, support and growth
   c. More organisations now form teams, using cell production as opposed to a traditional production line
   d. Team working occurs when production is organised into large units of work instead of by a high division of labour
   e. In a firm, there can be different types of teams: decision teams; knowledge teams; and work teams
   f. Decision team:
      i. This comprises management.
      ii. Its main function is to make decisions about the operation of the firm.
   g. Knowledge team:
      i. This consists of work teams and decision teams.
      ii. The advantage of having this team is that it allows the firm to know the impact of a decision on all departments of the firm.
   h. Work team:
      i. This consists of workers who must work together to achieve a given objective.
      ii. It is essential that members of the team are multi-skilled.
   i. Characteristics of effective teams:
      i. Effective teams have a clear understanding of what their goals are.
      ii. Members of the team are committed to achieving their specific task.
      iii. Members of the team have the resources to achieve the given task.
      iv. Members of the team have established a level of trust.
      v. Members of the team can communicate effectively.

| Advantages and disadvantages of a team organisation structure | |
|---|---|
| **Advantages** | **Disadvantages** |
| › By working in teams, individuals can share:<br>o Skills<br>o Knowledge<br>o Experience | › It may take time for groups to agree on any given situation |
| › Are motivated by working with others (social needs) | › Some individuals may feel that others are not working hard enough and may not want to be part of the team |
| › It improves communication | › Some individuals cannot work in a team |
| › Better decision-making | › Team norms may be poor, if teams are allowed to develop poor work ethics |

6. **By network**
   a. Networks shows informal relationships.
   b. The relationships are determined by questionnaires.
   c. Social relationships and knowledge flows are established.
   d. Advantages include:
      i. Management can identify ways to improve the flow of information.
      ii. Identifying the individuals or groups that play a key role in the firm.
7. **By virtual organisation**
   a. Advances in media, technology and globalisation gave rise to virtual organisation.
   b. A virtual organisation is an organisation where its members are located in different geographical areas.
   c. The virtual organisation is therefore dependent on technology, e.g. the computer, email.

d. The firm may appear to have the characteristics of a normal traditional firm, but it differs in the way in which value is added.

e. The structure of such a firm is always changing. Firms that exhaust such a structure have few physical assets. It means therefore that adding value to the output is dependent more on technology, knowledge and less on physical plant and machinery.

f. Office space is not allocated to specific employees. They work wherever space is available.

| Advantages and disadvantages of virtual organisation structure | |
|---|---|
| **Advantages** | **Disadvantages** |
| › It is possible for the firm to have experts from any part of the word | › There is the possibility that productivity can fall for those workers who telecommute, i.e. work at home, if they become distracted by activities at home |
| › It creates employment in rural areas | › The firm can experience communication problems. Workers are recruited from various parts of the world where language and cultural factors may hinder effective communication |
| › Experiences less worker absenteeism as workers are working from home | |
| › Productivity increases as workers are in a stress-free environment | |
| › The firms profit margin would increase because:<br>o Workers are paid for their work completed and not for the stipulated hours of work.<br>o The firm can hire qualified workers from any part of the world where it is possible to pay them a lower wage<br>o Less cost for electricity, insurance, etc. | |
| › As productivity increases the firm can acquire a competitive advantage over other firms | |

g. Benefits to employees:
   i. They have more independence.
   ii. They make financial savings, in terms of transportation costs.
   iii. Workers are more independent: they can work where they need to.
   iv. Workers experience less stress than others: as they are working from home

h. Benefits society, since less transportation means less air pollution

# Characteristics of the formal organisational structure

**1. Hierarchy**
   a. The hierarchy establishes the order or level of the structure of the firm.
   b. Lower ranks are subordinate to higher ranks.
   c. A tall organisational structure has a large number in the hierarchy.

**2. Chain of command**
   a. The chain of command shows how authority is passed down within the organisation.
   b. Information passes upwards.

**3. Span of control**
   a. Span of control refers to the number of subordinates reporting directly to a manager.
   b. It can be wide, giving subordinates some decision-making power; this motivates.
   c. It can be narrow; this allows for improved communication, and closer supervision.

| Narrow span of control | Wide span of control |
|---|---|
| › There is a greater degree of supervision and control of workers<br>› The relationship between top management and workers at the lower level of the firm is stronger | › The distance between top management and workers at the bottom of the organisational structure will be smaller<br>› The communication between management and the workers at the lower level in the firm will be reduced |

| Advantages | Advantages |
| --- | --- |
| › Tighter supervisions of subordinates<br>› Mistakes cannot be made<br>› Less stress for each worker: scope of each job is limited<br>› More layers in the hierarchy, therefore more scope for promotion<br>› Improved communication between supervisors and subordinates | › There will be scope for delegation<br>› Delegation increases motivation<br>› Increased opportunity for promotion<br>› Managers are forced to delegate<br>› Subordinates are given greater responsibility for tasks<br>› There is less supervision of subordinates<br>› Fewer layers in the hierarchy means vertical communication is improved |
| Disadvantages | Disadvantages |
| › Supervisors are too closely involved in subordinates' work<br>› Cost is high: there are too many managers<br>› There is distance between the top of the firm and those at the bottom | › Loss of control is possible if managers are not efficient |

A narrow span of control          A wide span of control

Span of control

4. **Line and staff relationship**
   a. Line relationship: this shows the authority managers have over subordinates, i.e. communication passes downwards.
   b. Staff relationship: this establishes the link that exists between the different departments, e.g. personnel manager has to interact with every department.

5. **Responsibility**
   Employees must be held accountable for their actions or decisions they make.

6. **Authority**
   Whenever a task is delegated to an employee, they must be given the necessary authority to accomplish the task.

7. **Accountability**
   Whenever an employee is given the necessary authority to carry out a task, they must be accountable for the execution of that task.

8. **Delegation**
   a. Delegation involves passing down authority and responsibilities to workers lower down the hierarchy. The subordinate is given the authority to make decisions, but managers remain accountable for the decisions. The wider the span of control, the greater the degree of delegation.
   b. It is a motivational tool used by managers.
   c. For delegation to be effective, managers must ensure:
      i. The worker is competent to perform the given task.
      ii. All workers are aware of who has been given the specific authority.
      iii. That interesting tasks as well as less interesting tasks are delegated.
      iv. The worker has the responsibility and the necessary authority to accomplish the given tasks.
      v. That communication is two-way.

9. **Centralisation**
   a. Centralisation occurs where all the important decisions are made by the senior managers or head office. There is very little scope for delegation.

b. Centralised decision-making may result in:

    i.   Greater consistency in decision-making.

    ii.  Greater control over decision-making.

    iii. Possible economies of scale in relation to the employment of managers.

## 10. Decentralisation

a. Decentralisation involves responsibility and authority: decision-making is given to individual departments or lower level managers.

b. Managers have the authority to make some decisions, not the head office.

c. There is effective delegation.

d. The staff are empowered and motivated.

e. It allows for better decision-making.

f. This may result in:

    i.   Quicker decision-making

    ii.  Increased motivation for lower-level managers

    iii. Development of skills for lower-level managers.

g. The advantages must be balanced against the fact that it will be difficult for lower-level managers to have an understanding of how their decisions will impact on the entire firm.

| Advantages of decentralisation | Disadvantages of decentralisation |
| --- | --- |
| › Senior managers have more time for strategic planning | › A decentralised organisation is more difficult to control |
| › Attention can be placed on the firm's cost centres, e.g. giving individual managers a budget to control | › Employees would have more responsibility; some employees, Theory X workers, would not want this |
| › Administrative costs may be lower | |
| › Workers are more motivated | |
| › Junior managers are closer to the customer and can respond more quickly to customer requirements | |

 QUICK TEST

1. **State how organisations are classified.** [10 marks]
2. **Define chain of command.** [5 marks]
3. **Discuss the advantages and disadvantages of a narrow span of control.** [15 marks]
4. **What are the benefits and drawbacks to a named firm of a wide span of control?** [15 marks]
5. **Define delegation.** [5 marks]
6. **Discuss the advantages and disadvantages of delegation to a named firm.** [15 marks]

# Motivation

## Objectives

At the end of this section, you will know:

1. **Factors that influence motivation.**
2. **Examples of financial incentives.**
3. **Examples of non-financial incentives.**
4. **How managers can apply motivational theories to preserve their situation.**
5. **Maslow's Hierarchy of Needs.**
6. **Herzberg's Hygiene Theory.**

## Factors that stimulate and influence motivation

### Introduction

1. **The major factor that contributes to the success of any firm is the level of motivation that exists. Success depends on how much management and workers are motivated.**
2. **The following are some of the factors that motivate workers:**
   a. Pay and fringe benefits
   b. Working environment
   c. Opportunities for promotion
   d. Job security
   e. Status and prestige at work
   f. Interesting and challenging work
   g. Management style
   h. Personal relationships with other workers
   i. Terms and conditions of employment
   j. Social life
   k. Communication within the organisation

## Theories of motivation

1. **Abraham Maslow's Hierarchy of Needs**
   a. Maslow based his theory on a hierarchy of needs.
   b. The concept of hierarchy of needs has two consequences:
      i. Lower order needs must be satisfied first.
      ii. Once a need is satisfied, it no longer motivates. Only unmet needs motivate.

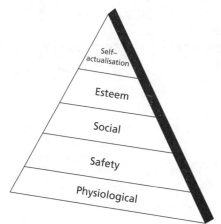

Maslow's hierarchy of needs

   c. Application of Maslow to present-day management:
      Maslow claimed that human needs consist of five types that he referred to as the hierarchy of needs:
      i. Physiological: good wage, salary structure, adequate working conditions.
      ii. Safety: security at work, pensions, a safe working environment.
      iii. Social: opportunities for teamwork, organising social events.
      iv. Esteem: creating opportunities for promotion.
      v. Self-actualisation: giving workers challenging, new tasks.

2. **Frederick Herzberg's Hygiene (two-factor) theory**

   a. Herzberg distinguished between **motivators**, which give positive satisfaction, and **hygiene** or **maintenance** factors.

   b. Maintenance factors do not give positive satisfaction but, if absent, will cause dissatisfaction.

   c. Maintenance factors are necessary conditions that must be present but are not a sufficient condition for motivation. These include:

      i. Job security; i.e. security of tenure.

      ii. Favourable working conditions.

      iii. Recognition.

      iv. Good relationship with all workers in the firm's hierarchy.

      v. Opportunities to interact with supervisors.

      vi. Opportunities to use their skills to the fullest.

      vii. Pay and wages.

      viii. Pension.

   d. Motivational factors are built into the job

      i. They motivate employees to improve their performance.

      ii. They include satisfying the following:

         1. Scope for advancement: social needs.

         2. Recognition: self-esteem needs.

         3. Greater responsibility: self-actualisation needs.

   e. Application of Herzberg to modern-day management:

      i. Create a healthy working environment for workers

      ii. Pay workers a fair salary/wage

      iii. Offer fringe benefits

      iv. Create opportunities for social interaction, e.g. family day.

3. **Other theories**

   a. **Elton Mayo: Human Relations School of Management**

      i. Hawthorne Studies: Mayo conducted research into groups at the Hawthorne works of the Western Electric Company between 1927 and 1932.

      ii. He focused on the workers' needs.

      iii. He made changes to working conditions.

      iv. Hawthorne workers found that output rose even when working conditions worsened.

      v. His conclusion:

         1. Workers had formed a tightly knit group.

         2. Workers enjoyed the attention paid to them.

         3. Workers experienced increased self-esteem.

         4. As a result workers increased their output.

         5. Even when working conditions worsened, it led to higher levels of productivity because workers formed close personal groups and liked the attention paid to them.

         6. He concluded that group morale and a sense of personal worth were the most important motivating factors.

      vii. Motivation depends on:

         1. Type of job being carried out.

         2. Type of supervision.

         3. Group relationship.

         4. Group morale.

         5. Individual sense of worth.

         6. Focusing on workers' needs.

      viii. Mayo's thoughts:

         1. Work is a group activity.

         2. Informal groups in the workplace have strong control over the habits and attitudes of the individual, to the extent that individual needs take second place to group needs.

         3. Group collaboration must be planned for and developed. If this is achieved, disruptions and stoppages will be reduced: productivity can be improved.

         4. Management should organise teamwork and develop cooperation.

      ix. Application of Elton Mayo to modern-day management:

         1. Put workers to work in groups and teams.

         2. Pay attention to workers; develop two-way communication.

         3. Involve workers in decision-making.

    x. The contribution of the Human Relations School (Mayo/Maslow):

      1. Place emphasis on the value and importance of the worker.

      2. Management must consider workers in making decisions.

      3. Behavioural management theory has led to the creation of employee assistance programmes.

      4. It has emphasised the need for an effective manager.

**b. F. W. Taylor: Scientific School of Management**

    i. To maximise productivity, use scientific management methods.

    ii. The worker is regarded as an 'Economic Animal', responding directly to financial incentives.

    iii. Workers who meet the standards should be rewarded with high pay.

    iv. His ideas are used in the concept of work study.

    v. Planning and directing should be left to those most capable, i.e. managers.

    vi. Workers should be left to follow instructions.

    vii. Specialisation of tasks; this increases productivity

      1. Worker's wages and standard of living would increase.

      2. Management: profit would increase as productivity increases.

    viii. Jobs should be standardised and simplified. These core elements should be distributed among workers according to their abilities, each of them performing one set of actions.

    ix. He developed **time and motion study**: tasks broken down into simple sub-tasks, which could be done quickly and monitored.

    x. Employees seek to maximise their own wealth.

    xi. To make workers work faster, required more money, i.e. Pay = Output

    xii. Payment by results using a piece-rate system.

    xiii. Jobs would become boring and repetitive.

**c. Douglas McGregor**

    i. McGregor's theory is essentially a theory of leadership.

    ii. The theory looks at how management view workers.

    iii. He established two opposing views of the psychological make-up of workers.

    iv. These views are classified as Theory X and Theory Y workers.

    v. Management who view their workers as Theory X, are likely to exhibit an authoritarian form of leadership; i.e. pay workers by results, supervise workers closely.

    vi. For workers who are perceived to be Theory Y, management would adopt a democratic form of leadership, which encourages two-way communication, and delegate responsibility to workers.

### Theory X workers vs. Theory Y workers

| Theory X workers | Theory Y workers |
| --- | --- |
| › Motivated by extrinsic factors: by money and threat of punishment | › Motivated by intrinsic factors: by a number of other factors not only money |
| › Are lazy, unambitious; not to be trusted | › Enjoy work |
| › Avoid responsibilities | › Seek responsibilities |
| › Require constant supervision | › Are self-motivated and can work on their own initiative |
| › Do not like change | › Welcome change |
| › Not concerned about the objectives of the firm or organisation | › Are flexible |
| **Effects of Theory X workers on leadership styles** | **Effects of Theory Y workers on leadership styles** |
| › Autocratic leadership<br>› Centralised decision-making<br>› Scientific Management | › Democratic leadership<br>› Decentralisation<br>› Various ways to motivate workers |

    vii. Application of McGregor's Theory X and Theory Y

    According to McGregor, the following will motivate workers:

      1. Money – for Theory X worker

      2. More supervision – for Theory X worker

      3. More responsibilities – for Theory Y worker

      4. More challenging tasks – for Theory Y worker

      5. Less supervision – for Theory Y worker

# Financial and non-financial motivational strategies

## Financial incentives

Financial methods of motivation include the following:

1. **Payment systems**
2. **Appraisal**
3. **Job evaluation**
4. **Work study**

1. **Payment systems**
   a. Piece rate:
      i. Workers are paid for each unit of output produced.
      ii. It may increase output at the expense of quality.
      iii. It is difficult to apply to the service industry.
   b. Profit-related pay:
      i. Workers get a share of the profit made.
      ii. It encourages employees to work hard to increase profits.
      iii. When demand for the firm's output falls, wages will fall, so redundancies may be avoided.
   c. Commission:
      i. It is a payment based on the value of the worker's sales.
      ii. It can form all or part of the worker's salary.
   d. Performance-related pay:
      i. It is related to an assessment of the employee's output.
      ii. It can have a negative effect on employee morale.
   e. Share ownership:
      i. Employees are offered shares in the company.
      ii. Shares can be purchased through savings schemes.
      iii. It can have a negative effect if shares are only available to senior managers.
   f. Fringe benefits:
      i. These are non-monetary forms of reward.
      ii. They are used in addition to pay.
      iii. They allow the firm to attract the best workers.
      iv. Some fringe benefits are not taxed. They include:
         1. Company cars
         2. Free insurance
         3. Discount on company products
         4. Low interest rate on loans.

2. **Appraisal:**
   a. Appraisal is conducted annually.
   b. It analyses workers' performance against pre-set targets.
   c. It is an intrinsic factor that can motivate workers.

3. **Job evaluation**
   a. Job evaluation is about comparing jobs.
   b. It allows for the creation of a wage structure that is fair.
   c. There are several strategies used to evaluate a job, but the point system is the one most frequently used.
   d. Job analysis gives a description of the job, the skills required, working conditions, value of assets the worker is responsible for.
   e. Relevant job factors are then identified: skills, qualifications, responsibility, working conditions.
   f. Points are allocated to each job. Points are then totalled. To total, determine the rank order of the job for pay determination.

## 4. Work study

   a. Work study is a technique used by F. W. Taylor.

   b. It involves the study of a particular task with the objective of redesigning it to make production more efficient.

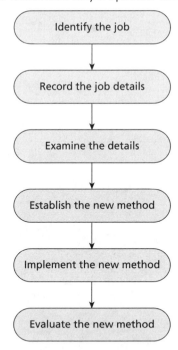

Steps in work study

   c. Work study consists of:

      i. Method study

      ii. Work measurement.

## 5. Method study

   a. The objectives of method study are to:

      1. Avoid bottlenecks

      2. Reduce levels of waste

      3. Increase machinery utilisation.

   b. Method study uses time and motion study.

   c. All measurements and tasks are recorded in detail.

   d. Method study looks at the methods to be employed in production.

   e. If several workers are doing the same job, each worker is given a rating.

   f. A basic time is then established. This is based on the time taken by an average worker to complete the task.

   g. Targets can then be set for each worker according to their rating.

   h. Employees with a higher rating can be given a higher than average target, with increased pay.

   i. There is a best method of doing a job. Study the job and the best method will be established.

## 6. Work measurement:

   a. Work measurement is the technique used to establish how long the task should take to complete.

   b. It uses the concept of standard time and standard performance:

      1. Standard time: the time it takes for a competent worker to complete a task.

      2. Standard performance: the average output rate of a competent worker, using agreed production methods.

   c. Time study: a stop watch is used to determine the time taken for a qualified worker to complete a task.

   d. Activity sampling: observing workers and the time taken on tasks.

   e. Standard data: using secondary data for previous measurements to establish the time for the new job.

   f. Predetermined motion time system: uses table for the time taken to carry out basic movements.

   g. The main methods used to measure work:

   h. Observation

   i. Synthetic methods.

# Non-financial incentives

**Non-financial incentives include:**

> **Delegation**
> **Quality circles**
> **Job enrichment**
> **Job enlargement**
> **Team working and empowerment**
> **Participation**
> **Promotion and job satisfaction.**

1. **Delegation and empowerment:**
   a. Delegation and empowerment is the passing of authority down the hierarchy.
   b. Workers are given the opportunity to make some decisions.
   c. They are given the authority and responsibility.
   d. Delegation is an important part of democratic leadership.
   e. It can provide employees with a greater satisfaction from their work.

2. **Quality circles:**
   a. Quality circles consist of a group of workers drawn from all levels within the organisation.
   b. They meet regularly to identify methods of improving all aspects of the quality of the products.
   c. Employees therefore contribute to decision-making.
   d. Employees are motivated.
   e. Management gain insight to solving production problems.
   f. It allows the worker to improve the nature of the work they are doing.

3. **Job enrichment:**
   a. Job enrichment gives employees greater responsibility.
   b. It increases the complexity of the task they perform.
   c. It gives workers authority.
   d. Workers can use their abilities to the fullest.
   e. Herzberg pointed out that enriched jobs should contain a range of tasks and challenges for the worker at different ability levels and provide opportunities for achievement and feedback on performance.
   f. Job enrichment requires training.
   g. It vertically extends workers' participation.
   h. It allows workers to become more productive.
   i. Workers feel they are rewarded for their contribution to the firm.
   j. It may be an asset: may lead to future promotion.

4. **Job enlargement/horizontal loading:**
   a. Job enlargement or horizontal loading gives employees additional tasks of a similar level of complexity.
   b. There is less repetition and monotony.
   c. It expands the jobs horizontally.

5. **Team working and empowerment:**
   a. Team working and empowerment allows employees to:
      i. Plan their own work
      ii. Make their own decisions
      iii. Solve their own problems
      iv. Achieve some of their higher needs: according to Maslow or Herzberg.
   b. Advantages:
      i. Lower labour turnover
      ii. Product quality improved.

6. **Participation:**
   a. Here workers are involved in decision-making.
   b. This can occur at team formation, or at the individual level.
   c. Opportunities for participation, e.g. how to improve quality.
   d. Giving workers the opportunity to elect a worker representative on the various committees with management.

---

 QUICK TEST

1. **State the factors that influence motivation** [5 marks]
2. **Explain Maslow's Hierarchy of Needs** [15 marks]
3. **Apply Herzberg's Hygiene Theory to a named firm.** [10 marks]
4. **State the various financial incentives a named firm can use to motivate its workers.** [15 marks]
5. **Discuss the various non-financial incentives a firm can use to motivate workers.** [15 marks]

# Leadership

## Objectives

At the end of this section, you will know:

1. **The following leadership theories:**
   a. McGregor's Theory X and Theory Y
   b. Trait theory
2. **The skills a leader must have.**
3. **The various leadership styles.**
4. **The advantages and disadvantages of informal leadership.**

**Leadership style** refers to the way in which managers make decisions and relate to their staff.

## Leadership theory: McGregor's Theory X and Theory Y

### Douglas McGregor

He outlined two opposing views about the psychological characteristics of workers: Theory X and Theory Y.

| Assumptions about workers | |
|---|---|
| **Theory X** | **Theory Y** |
| › Lazy | › Can enjoy work |
| › Unambitious | › Enjoys responsibility |
| › Dislike change | › Wants to develop self |
| › Need coercion | › Prepared to adapt |
| › Need close supervision | › Capable of working on own initiative |
| › Motivated by money | |
| › Ignores the needs of the firm | |

## The trait theory

1. **It is a genetic approach to understanding leadership. It assumes that leaders are born rather than made.**
2. **It assumes the following traits are necessary for managerial success:**
   › Superior intelligence
   › Imposing stature
   › Self-confidence
   › Effectiveness in communication
   › Ability to motivate others
   › The need for achievement
   › Decisiveness
   › Creativity
3. **The theory is not widely accepted today. The major difficulty with this approach is that being a genetically based theory, it does not assume that traits are learned.**
4. **Many leadership traits, e.g. communication skills can be learnt.**
5. **It is used, however, in some employee-performance-appraisal systems.**

## Leadership skills

Leadership skills include the following:

i. **Adaptability**
ii. **Tact**
iii. **Communication**
iv. **Problem solving**
v. **Critical thinking**
vi. **Listening**

## Leadership styles

### Autocratic leadership style

1. **Authoritarian and assumes responsibility for all aspects of the firm's operations.**
2. **Communication is one way – from top to bottom.**
3. **There is a clear chain of command.**

4. **Decision-making is quick.**
5. **This style of leadership creates frustration and resentment.**
6. **Workers become dependent on the leader.**
7. **Leader retains control.**
8. **It gives rise to dissatisfaction with the leader.**
9. **An autocratic leadership style is essential in some situations, where quick decisions are needed, e.g. police, fire service; a symphony orchestra is conducted by an autocratic leader.**

## Democratic/participative

1. **Communication is two-way.**
2. **Can be persuasive: leader makes the decision and convinces workers that the decision was good.**
3. **Can be consultative: where workers are consulted before a decision is made.**
4. **Leader strives for mutual understanding.**
5. **Gives rise to improved decisions.**
6. **Greater commitment.**
7. **Improved morale.**
8. **Time-consuming.**
9. **Appropriate where experienced workers need to be fully involved in their work.**

## Laissez Faire

1. **The leader has a peripheral role, leaving the staff to manage the firm.**
2. **Leader evades his responsibilities: he delegates it.**
3. **Communication is horizontal.**
4. **Can bring out the best if workers are professionals.**
5. **However, staff may lack focus: dissatisfaction may occur.**
6. **Numerous discussions add unnecessary costs to the firm.**
7. **Decision-making takes longer.**

## Transformational leader

1. **A leader who has the vision, the power and the personality to effect the change necessary to bring about radical changes in the firm.**
2. **Must be able to inspire other members in the firm to work with them to achieve the stated objective.**
3. **Must be a role model and able to promote cooperation and harmony among staff.**

**Informal leaders** are individuals who have the ability to lead without formal power.

### Informal leadership

This may be because of their experiences, personalities or knowledge

| Informal leadership | |
| --- | --- |
| **Advantages** | **Disadvantages** |
| › They may have more knowledge on special issues than the formal leaders | › They have the ability to lead workers – sometimes in the wrong direction |
| › Management could work with them in order to improve the relationship between management and workers | › They may cause friction in the workplace if their views are different from those of management |
| › They can help management implement policies | › Their presence can give rise to negative informal groups in the firm |
| | › Output would fall, productivity would fall |

QUICK TEST

1. **State the skills necessary for good leadership** [10 marks]
2. **Identify the key features of:**
   a. Autocratic leadership style [10 marks]
   b. Democratic leadership style [10 marks]
3. **State the advantages and disadvantages of informal leadership as they relate to a named organisation** [15 marks]

# Group and team management

## Objectives

At the end of this section, you will know the:

1. **Stages of group development.**
2. **Characteristics of effective teams.**
3. **Factors that influence group cohesiveness.**
4. **Advantages and disadvantages of the teams in a firm.**

> **There are decision teams and work teams in business.**
> **Decision teams make decisions**
> **Work teams work to accomplish goals**

> A team is a group of people with a common aim.

> An effective team must possess the following characteristics: trust, commitment, participation, flexibility, decision by consensus, encouragement, support and growth.

## Stages of team development

There are a number of stages a group must go through before they are fully formed.
These are as follows:

1. **Forming: individuals in the group begin to know the members of the group.**
2. **Storming: conflict may arise if people's goals are different from each other and they may not want to accept someone else's point of view.**
3. **Norming: members begin to develop techniques to work together. Rules are established. Communication is improved.**
4. **Performing: the group begin to function effectively. Objectives are accomplished.**
5. **Adjourning: the group break up as the objectives are met, or because members have left.**

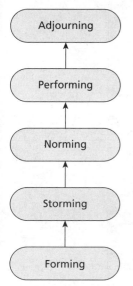

Stages of team development:

## The characteristics of effective teams

i. **Commitment**
  1. Each member of the team must know they are valuable to the team.
  2. They must know that the aims and objectives of the team are in keeping with their own perspectives.
  3. Each team member is willing to work with other team members.
ii. **Participation**
  1. Each member of the team must feel confident enough to participate in discussions.
  2. Each member must be given the opportunity to express a point of view.
iii. **Trust**
  1. Managers must have the belief that team members are well trained to achieve their objectives.
  2. Give to the teams the necessary responsibility and the authority that goes with it.
iv. **Decisions by consensus**
  > The findings of the team must be the consensus of the entire team.
v. **Flexibility**
  1. Teams must be able to make quick decisions in response to any given situation.
  2. Team members might be more willing to fill in for an absent team member.

vi. **Encouragement**
  › Each member of the team must be able to encourage each other.

vii. **Support and growth**
  1. Senior management must support teams.
  2. Provide the necessary training and resources necessary for growth.

## Factors that influence group cohesiveness

i. **Size:**
  1. The ideal size may be about five persons, but the size of the group is determined by the task.
  2. However, no universally accepted group size ensures maximum efficiency.

ii. **The following guidelines may be considered:**
  1. A group should not be too small: it should have enough individuals to accomplish the task.
  2. Groups that are too large lead to impersonal relationships: the ideal group size allows members to rely on each other, and allow for group cohesiveness.
  3. Members should feel obligated to the group: too large a group prevents this.

iii. **Group goals**
  Each member of the group must aim to achieve the group goals.

| Teams | |
|---|---|
| **Advantages to the organisation** | **Disadvantages to the organisation** |
| › Productivity is increased because of the pooling of ideas | › The introduction of team working will require workers to be trained to work as a group. There is a financial cost to the firm |
| › It reduces management cost: there will be less need for middle management | › Time is lost: production is disrupted as teams establish themselves |
| › There is continuity: if a member of a team is absent, others can continue to function | › More time is taken to arrive at a decision as there are more members in the team |
| › New teams can be formed as the needs of the organisation changes | › If some of the members of the team are more vocal than others, decision-making will not be effective, as other members may feel left out and will not contribute |
| › People can specialise and benefit from the skill and knowledge of team members | › Teams may develop values that conflict with those of the organisation |
| › Responsibility is shared | › It can result in the loss of specialisation among workers |
| › They are better able to solve different business problems | |
| › Workers are more motivated; fewer accidents on the job; less labour turnover; fewer negative informal groups | |
| › There is the sharing of ideas and the pooling of expertise from each team member; this leads to better decision-making | |

 QUICK TEST

1. **What is a team?**  [ 5 marks]
2. **State the characteristics of an effective team.**  [15 marks]
3. **State the advantages of teams to a named firm.**  [10 marks]
4. **State the disadvantages of teams to a named firm.**  [10 marks]

# Causes of conflict

## Objective

At the end of this section, you will know the causes of conflict in a firm.

In any organisation conflict will occur between individuals. Conflict can be healthy and lead to growth or have the opposite effect.

## Possible causes of conflict

The following are possible causes of conflict:

a. **Management style**

Conflict between management and workers occurs:

i. If management style is generally autocratic.

ii. If there is a clear distinction between management and workers, i.e. 'us vs. them'.

iii. If workers feel their views are not important.

b. **Competition for scarce resources**

i. The demand for the firm's resources will be greater than the supply of resources.

ii. There will be conflict as various departments each will feel the resources given to them will not allow them to achieve their objectives.

c. **Lack of communication**

i. If management is autocratic, communication is downward; workers cannot express their views, so conflict will arise.

ii. Conflict can also arise if the firm does not have well-established, clear communication systems.

d. **Clash of personalities**

This occurs when workers cannot see another person's point of view, and no one wants to back-down; for example, between management and trade union representatives.

 QUICK TEST

1. State the possible causes of conflict in a named firm       **[10 marks]**
2. Discuss the reasons why employees in a named firm may resist change       **[10 marks]**

# Strategies to manage conflict

## Objectives

At the end of this section, you will know the strategies to deal with conflict in a firm.

**a. Avoidance**
   i.   This strategy might be used if the issue causing the conflict is not very significant.
   ii.  Management can ignore it.

**b. Smoothing**
   i.   This occurs when one of the persons on the team is in the conflict and makes every effort to avoid further conflict by accommodating the other side.
   ii.  Management does not place emphasis on the conflict.
   iii. This strategy will work only where issues are not very significant.

**c. Compromise**
   i.   This is where both parties agree that a compromise situation will benefit both parties, i.e. middle ground.
   ii.  This approach is used when a temporary solution is needed for work to continue.

**d. Collaboration**
   i.   This involves both parties in the dispute coming together to resolve the issue.
   ii.  There is open discussion, a general understanding of each other's point of view and a mutual agreement is reached.

**e. Confrontation**
   i.   This strategy is used:
        1.  If a quick resolution is needed.
        2.  If there is a struggle for power between opposing sides, where one party wins and the other loses.
   ii.  The objective is to justify the position taken to resolve the conflict.

---

 QUICK TEST

1. **State the strategies a named firm can use to manage conflict.**          **[15 marks]**
2. **When would each of the above named strategies be used?**          **[10 marks]**

# Management of change

## Objectives

At the end of this section, you will know:

1. **The nature of change**
2. **Why workers resist change**
3. **Strategies that can be used to manage change**

## Nature of change

i. **Technological change has led to:**

1. The way in which the firm operates.
2. High cost of purchasing the technology.
3. High cost of training workers.
4. More efficient methods of keeping records.
5. More efficient methods of communication.

ii. **Economic change**

1. Management has also to deal with changes in the economic external environment.
2. Changes in the trade cycle means:
   › Consumers' disposable income changes.
   › Tax rates may change.
   › Exchange rates change.
   › Demand for output changes.
3. These will require management to rethink its policies on: expansion, level of output.

iii. **Demographic changes**

As the size and structure of the population change, so too must the way the firm operates.

iv. **Social changes**

As the structure of the society changes, management must keep abreast of these changes; for example, more working women will mean the demand for appropriate working clothing will increase, and the demand for pre-cooked and fast food will also increase.

v. **Legal**

1. Firms will also have to deal with legal issues; e.g. methods of advertising, minimum wages, health and safety regulations.
2. Firms may have to change their advertising technique; take some products off the market.

## Resistance to change

i. **Fear**

Workers resist change because of the following fears:

1. They may lose their jobs.
2. Their friends may lose their jobs.

ii. **Disrupted habits**

1. Workers may be forced to:
   a. Adopt new methods of working.
   b. Adopt different working hours.
2. This would put added strain on the worker.

iii. **Loss of control and confidence**

Workers may lose confidence in themselves because:

1. They have to learn new methods for completing a given task. Some workers may feel they are too old to be retrained.
2. They may feel they have lost control if the firm employs a new management system and the worker loses some of their own responsibilities.
3. The firm is taken over by another firm and the worker's workload is shared.

iv. **Poor training**

Workers would resist change:

1. If they feel they lack the necessary training.
2. If they are not given the opportunity to acquire the necessary training.

v. **Redistribution of workload and lack of purpose**

1. Redistribution of workload
   a. Workers may resist change if they feel the change would give them more responsibilities.
   b. If they perceive other workers would have less work.

2. Lack of purpose:
   a. If workers feel the change was not necessary, they may resist any attempts to execute change.
   b. If the cost of the change is greater than the benefits to the worker, they will resist change.

**vi. Loss of power**
If workers feel they have no control over their jobs and are losing power, they would resist change.

**vii. Lack of communication**
Workers would resist change if the method of communicating the change was not effective, that is, communication is downward and workers did not have an input in the decision.

## Strategies to manage change

1. **Management must be clear on its objectives for bringing about the proposed change and must be able to see the change implemented.**
2. **Management must ensure that morale in the workforce is high. If this is so, then the proposed change will be more readily accepted.**
3. **There must be a level of trust; if workers know they will benefit from the proposed change, they will be more likely to accept this change.**
4. **Management must provide the necessary training to equip workers so they will feel comfortable in the changed environment.**
5. **Management must introduce change gradually, wherever this is possible.**
6. **There must be open communication about the proposed change. All stakeholders must be free to express their point of view.**
7. **It is important that those affected by the proposed change are given sufficient time to adjust to the change.**

Compromise is vital in the strategy to manage change. Wherever possible, management must listen to the concerns of those who will be affected by the change and if workers know that they are important, it is more likely they will accept the proposed change

 QUICK TEST

1. State the various factors that can bring about change in a named firm.          [15 marks]
2. Give reasons why workers may resist change in a named firm.                     [15 marks]
3. Discuss the strategies management can use to manage change.                     [15 marks]

# Communication in business

## Objectives

At the end of this section, you will know:

1. **What is effective communication**
2. **The various channels of communication**
3. **The lines of communication**
4. **The problems associated with the formal channels**

Communication is said to be effective when what is said is understandable in the way it was intended and there is feedback.

### a. Effective communication

1. Management's main objective is to get things done through others. This means letting people know what they have to do, listening to them and noting their progress.
2. To communicate effectively, management must:
   › Obtain feedback
   › **Empathise**: this means they must try to see things from the other person's point of view and they must use the language that will be understood.
   › **Consider the external environment**: if there is noise or anything else in the external environment that would prevent the receiver from understanding the message correctly.
   › **Use the most appropriate channel of communication**:
      o Face-to-face communication allows for the additional use of body language
      o Written communication is more effective for more detailed information
      o One-way communication is faster and better for use in the military but inadequate elsewhere.

### b. Effective two-way communication can improve productivity:

1. According to Mayo, it is important for managers to show they are interested in the welfare of their employees.
2. Communication can meet the social and esteem needs of the worker.
3. Hertzberg noted that feedback is an important motivator.

### c. Effective communication and motivation:

1. Motivation is important for the success of the firm. To motivate employees, it is vital to communicate information effectively to them and to obtain feedback on their performance.
2. This is a two-way process.
3. The more motivated worker is more likely to communicate.

Motivation and communication

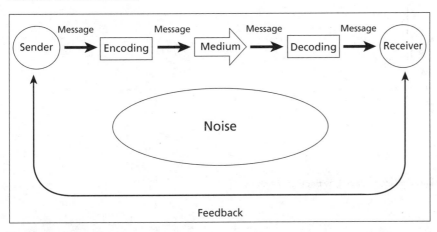

The communication process

d. **Good communication in a firm**

When communication is good in a firm:

1. Messages do not get distorted.
2. Information is passed quickly and effectively, enabling improved decision-making.
3. There is both upward and downward communication.
4. Information flows effectively between the firm and the external environment.

# Communication structure

1. **All communication takes place in formal or informal networks.**
2. **Formal communication is linked to the firm's organisational structure. It shows the lines of authority and the relationship between departments or functions. It also shows formal communication networks that exist in the firm.**
3. **The wheel**
   a. For simple tasks, the wheel is more efficient and accurate than the chain or the circle.
   b. The wheel has a central pattern; therefore the group cannot adapt to changed circumstances.
   c. One person is at the centre.
   d. That person can communicate with other group members.
   e. All communication must pass through the person at the centre.

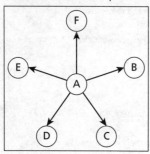

The wheel

4. **The chain**
   a. The chain is the slowest and the least effective.
   b. Information is passed from one person to another in the group.
   c. It is based on the existing chains of command within the firm. Communication flows from superior to subordinates along the chain.
   d. This network is associated with a 'tall' structure and authoritarian organisation; e.g. police, military.

The chain

5. **The circle**
   a. The circle is superior.
   b. The circle satisfies group members.
   c. It can adapt to changing situations.
   d. Communication is circular.
   e. Information passes from one person to another.

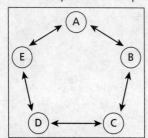

The circle

6. **All channels**

Every member in the group can communicate directly with other members.

# Communication channels and communication methods

1. **There are different channels used in communication. These include:**
    i. Oral
    ii. Written
    iii. Visual
    iv. Non-verbal.

2. **Methods of communication include:**
    i. Internet
    ii. Email
    iii. Intranet
    iv. Face-to-face
    v. Video conferencing.
    **Note: All communication channels and methods can be used internally (in the firm) and externally (outside the firm).**

3. **Types of communication include:**
    i. Internal
    ii. External
    iii. Formal
    iv. Informal
    v. One-way
    vi. Two-way

4. **Internal communication (within the firm):**

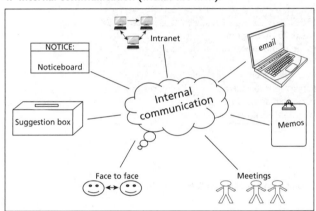

Internal communication

# Lines of communication

Formal and informal communication channels can exist in the firm.

i. **Formal channel: vertical and horizontal**
    1. Formal channels of communication are recognised by the firm as its method of passing information to the workforce; e.g. meetings, noticeboards.
    2. Formal communication channels are indicated by the firm's formal structure (chain of command and span of control).
    3. Formal channels can be vertical or horizontal.
    4. Vertical communication is downward or upward:
        a. Downward communication: when information passes down the hierarchy from managers to subordinates, e.g. instructions.
        b. Upward communication; this occurs where information passes from subordinates to managers.
        c. Horizontal communication: members of a team communicate with each other at team meetings or through issuing memos.

ii. **Informal channels: grapevine, groups**
    › Informal channels are not recognised by the firm; e.g, the grapevine.
    › They allow for two-way communication.
    › These coexist with the formal channels.
    › These are based on friendship and recognition.
    › They assume greater importance where the formal networks are not working efficiently.

>    › They transmit information quickly in firms with tall structures.
>    › The quality of the communication is influenced by the subjective judgements of those transmitting the information.

**iii. Problems associated with formal channels**
1. Record of the communication is kept. This may deter people from expressing their views for fear that it could be used against them later.
2. There may not be the opportunity for feedback.
3. It takes time to organise, e.g. meetings, reports.
4. Communication is restricted to people who are part of the channel.

**iv. Formal channel vs. informal channel**

| Formal channel | Informal channel |
| --- | --- |
| › Official<br>› Has authority and responsibility<br>› Established by management<br>› Established by rules | › Not official<br>› Based on power<br>› Group gives the power<br>› Established by norms |
| **Effective usage** | **Effective usage** |
| › Formal communication is used in the following situations:<br>  o Health and safety regulations<br>  o Employment contracts<br>  o Termination of contracts<br>  o Annual meetings with shareholders | › Informal channels can be used where:<br>  o Information needs to be sent quickly<br>  o It is used by managers to gain staff opinions on matters before making it formal<br>  o People are more likely to express their feelings through the informal channel |
|  | **Benefits** |
|  | › Less work for management<br>› Improved communication: faster movement of information<br>› Safety value for employees<br>› Greater cooperation: staff more likely to express themselves in an informal setting<br>› Motivation through working in groups |

## Barriers to effective communication

**i. Selective perceptions**

Selective perceptions occur when the receiver interprets information transmitted differently from the intended meaning. This may be due to cultural or personal factors.

**ii. Attitudes**

The attitude of the sender or receiver may be a barrier to effective communication:
a. If there is a lack of trust
b. If workers feel alienated

**iii. Noise**

Any noise in the internal environment, e.g. noise from machines, or in the external environment, such as rain or the sound of thunder, will have a negative effect on the quality or the way the message is received.

**iv. Cultural bias**

a. Cultural bias means interpreting communication based on one's culture, e.g. beliefs, expectations, social or economic background, or language.
b. Because of these cultural differences, the sender and the receiver may not understand each other.

## Factors affecting communication:

Four main factors affect effective communication:

1. **The transmitter**
2. **The message**
3. **The medium used**
4. **The receiver.**

i. **The transmitter**
   › Uses inaccurate technical terms.
   › Uses specialist vocabulary to new specialist.
   › Uses inappropriate language, e.g. jargon.
   › Gives too much information at the same time.
   › Uses unsuitable or inappropriate non-verbal communication to support the message.

ii. **The message**
   › Is sent over a long distance, inappropriate, non-direct methods.
   › Through a long chain of command, resulting in the message being transmitted through too many people and levels.
   › Too much information is transmitted at the same time.
   › Between a sender and a receiver of unequal status; one person may refuse to listen to the other party's message.

iii. **The medium**
   › Unsuitable for the information being transmitted.
   › Too slow in getting the message to the recipient in time for it to be acted upon.

iv. **The receiver**
   › Is not interested in the subject matter.
   › Interprets the message in an incorrect way because of personal bias, or wish to hear something else.
   › Is in an unsuitable physical or emotional state to receive the message accurately.
   › Receives a message that has been filtered, i.e. the information transmitted has been altered to make it appear more favourable to the receiver.

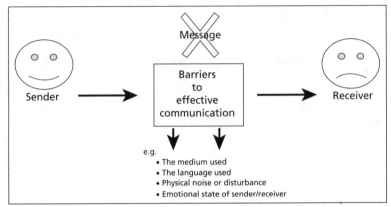

Barriers to effective communication

## Reducing barriers to communication

Strategies to overcome barriers to effective communication include:

1. **If the barrier is the sender:**
   a. The message should be short.
   b. The message should be clear.
   c. The language must be understood by the receiver.
   d. There must be feedback.

2. **If the wrong medium is used:**
   a. Always ensure feedback.
   b. Select the appropriate channel.
   c. The shorter the channel, the more effective it could be.
   d. Check if there is a breakdown in transmitting the message, e.g. computer failure, telephone malfunction, etc.

3. **If the barrier is the receiver:**
   a. Establish trust with the receiver.
   b. Ask for feedback.
   c. Ensure receiver has an interest in the subject matter.

## Problems of communication in larger organisations

1. As a firm grows it tends to have more employees and operates in more markets. This can create even more communication problems. For example:
   a. **Culture**: Parts of the firm may have their own culture and different ways of doing things that may conflict with other areas; individuals may not communicate effectively with other departments.
   b. **Alienation**: If employees do not feel part of the overall firm, communication will not flow easily. This can create an 'us and them' feeling among workers.
   c. **Geographical separation**: face-to-face communication becomes difficult to achieve.
   d. **Overload**:
      i. Managers may have a communication overload as too much information is being received. They may be unable to process it effectively. Feedback will be slow and may not be provided for some questions asked.
      ii. Communication can be more difficult as a firm grows.
2. As firms grow, therefore, management must employ information technology, alter the organisational structure and establish more teams and committees to ensure communication is effective.

## Overcoming communication problems in larger organisations

As the firm expands, communication becomes more difficult. The following are some strategies the firm can employ:
   a. **Decentralisation**: in a decentralised organisation local managers can make decisions without going up the hierarchy. This makes decision-making easier.
   b. **Using more information and communications technology**: the use of email, the internet, and fax, can connect different parts of the firm. This makes communication more effective.
   c. **Cross-functional teams**: teams of people from different departments can share information and show how problems may be dealt with from different points of view.
   d. **Delayering**: removing layers of the hierarchy makes for more effective communication. There is less opportunity for messages to be distorted.

## Management's role in effective communication

1. Management is about getting things done by giving instruction to workers. It involves telling workers what to do, listening to them and evaluating their progress.
2. To communicate effectively management must:
   a. **Empathise**: they must try to see things from other people's point of view. Choose the appropriate language and body language
   b. **Consider the environment**: ensure there are no distractions that may distort the message.
   c. **Obtain feedback**: ensure there is feedback.
   d. **Select the appropriate channel**: face-to-face communication can be effective. It allows for immediate feedback and is enforced by body language, but is not effective for detailed and sensitive information

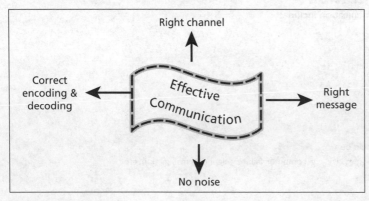

Effective communication

3. **Communication problems can be improved if managers:**
   a. Avoid giving too much information at the same time.
   b. Recognise that cultural and linguistic differences exist among workers.
   c. Ensure that all workers understand the objectives of the firm.
   d. Train employees in communication skills.
   e. Review the leadership style, allowing for more feedback.

4. **Management would then benefit from:**
   a. Improved decision-making
   b. More motivated employees
   c. Increased involvement in the firm
   d. A more coordinated approach

## QUICK TEST

1. **What is effective communication?**                                                    [5 marks]
2. **What are the various communication channels?**                                         [15 marks]
3. **State the various methods of communication.**                                          [10 marks]
4. **What are the problems associated with the formal channels of communication?**          [10 marks]
5. **What are the problems associated with the informal channels of communication?**        [10 marks]
6. **What are the barriers to effective communication?**                                    [10 marks]
7. **State the measures a named firm can use to ensure more effective communication.**       [15 marks]

# Human resources management

## Objectives

At the end of this section, you will know:

1. The functions of the human resource department
2. How to evaluate the success of the human resource department

## The role of human resource management in an organisation

1. Human resource management is the process of making the most efficient use of the human resources in the firm.
2. This is necessary in order for the firm to achieve its objectives. It involves management of the human resource in the following areas:
   a. Recruitment
   b. Selection
   c. Compensation
   d. Training and development
   e. Performance appraisal
   f. Managing change
3. In large organisations a human resources department is established. In smaller organisations these functions are performed by the respective heads of departments.
4. The human resources department is responsible for attracting, developing and maintaining an effective workforce.
5. It is vital for the human resources department to measure or assess worker performance. Improvements in performance should be noted and, more importantly, be communicated to staff. These include:
   a. Labour productivity
   b. Absenteeism rates
   c. Labour turnover
   d. Health and Safety
6. Labour productivity:
   a. Labour productivity compares the number of workers with total output.
   b. If it increases, labour is more efficient, and the firm will be more competitive as the cost of production is falling.
      Formula:

   $$\text{Labour productivity} = \frac{\text{Output per period}}{\text{Number of employees at work}}$$

7. Absenteeism rates:
   a. Absenteeism rates measure the proportion of the workforce who are ill, but who are absent over a given time period.
   b. Absenteeism can have the following consequences:
      i. Firms unable to meet targets
      ii. Loss of market share
      iii. Extra cost to hire workers to provide cover for absentees
      iv. Loss of morale
         Formula:

   $$\text{Absenteeism \%} = \frac{\text{Number of staff absent (on 1 day)} \times 100}{\text{Total number of staff}}$$

8. Labour turnover:
   a. Labour turnover measures the rate at which staff leave the firm.
   b. If it is high, it could be due to:
      i. Workers not satisfied with the style of management
      ii. There are low levels of motivation
      iii. The job has become too stressful
      iv. Better jobs opportunities elsewhere
      v. Scope for promotion is limited.

   c. Effect of high labour turnover:

     i. Cost to recruit workers

     ii. Cost to train workers

     iii. Customer service will suffer

     iv. May affect production targets

     v. Affects the image of the firm.

   d. It is possible that a high labour turnover will create the opportunity for the firm to employ workers who bring in new ideas.

   e. It may be possible for the firm to introduce new technologies to replace labour where this is possible:

   f. The effect of greater efficiency:

     i. Lower cost of production

     ii. Lower selling price

     iii. Increases the firm's competitiveness

     iv. Increase market share

     v. Increase profit margin

     vi. Leading to growth and expansion.

     Formula:

$$\text{Labour turnover \%} = \frac{\text{Number of staff leaving during the year} \times 100}{\text{Average number of staff}}$$

## 9. Health and safety

   a. Health and safety measures the number of working days lost for health and safety reasons.

   b. This is an important indication. Workers need to feel safe on the job. This will:

     i. Lower the number of sick days taken

     ii. Increase worker productivity

     iii. Lower cost to the firm in terms of:

       1. Downtime if work had to be stopped to deal with injured worker

       2. Reduce/eliminate money to be given as compensation for the injured worker

       3. Reduce possible legal cost, if health and safety regulations were not upheld

     iv. Lead to possible industrial problems

     Formula:

$$\text{Health and Safety \%} = \frac{\text{Number of working days lost per annum for health and safety reasons} \times 100}{\text{Total number of possible working days}}$$

## 10. Labour supply shortage

Labour supply shortages can be overcome by:

   a. Increasing mechanisation

   b. Retraining workers

   c. Offering workers greater incentives, better terms and conditions of employment

   d. Outsourcing

   e. Increasing overtime.

## Workforce planning

**1. Workforce planning involves forecasting the future demand for human resources in the firm. It involves:**

   a. Identifying the demand for human resources in the short-, medium- and long-term.

   b. Keeping personnel records up to date.

   c. Forecasting must be an important part of the strategic plan of the firm.

   d. Forecasts must be constantly updated.

   e. External factors should be taken into account, e.g. population trends, government policies.

**2. Ineffective human resource forecasting can result in:**

   a. High costs

   b. Redundancies

   c. High levels of labour turnover

   d. High levels of absenteeism

   e. Low morale

   f. Workers not well trained.

3. **It is one of the central activities of human resource management. A number of factors influence managers' decisions:**
   a. Firm's overall objectives
   b. Marketing and production objectives to determine
   c. Number and skills of workers required
   d. Financial position of the business
   e. State of the market and the economy.

## Functions of human resources department

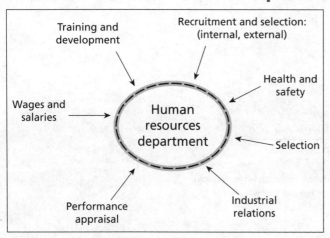

Functions of human resources department

## Recruitment

1. **There are two basic methods of recruiting staff:**
   a. Internally
   b. Externally.
2. **The method of recruitment will depend on:**
   a. Locating the jobs
   b. Cost
   c. Supply of labour
   d. Size of the organisation
   e. Historic factors.
3. **Internal recruitment:**
   Jobs may be advertised internally by using noticeboards, newsletter, etc.

| Internal recruitment | |
|---|---|
| **Advantages** | **Disadvantages** |
| › The person appointed already knows the working environment | › The firm does not benefit from the possibility of new ideas from someone coming from outside the firm |
| › More likely to remain in the job than a new employee | › It may cause internal conflict and resentment among those who did not approve of the firm's appointment |
| › It motivates staff morale | › Choice is limited; an unsuitable person may be selected |
| › It is quicker than external recruitment | |
| › It is cheaper | |

4. **External recruitment:**
   The advantages and disadvantages of external recruitment are essentially the opposite of internal recruitment.
5. **Methods of external recruitment:**
   a. Personal recommendation
   b. Government agencies
   c. Newspapers
   d. Professional journals
   e. Recruitment agencies
   f. Schools, universities
   g. Individuals who randomly apply for a position although none was advertised; firms keep these applications on file for the future.

## Selection
This includes the advertising of jobs, application process, interviews and testing.

1. **Job advertising**
   a. The job will be advertised giving the necessary details of the vacant position and the terms and condition of employment.
   b. For example:
      i. job title
      ii. work involved
      iii. earnings
      iv. fringe benefits
      v. holidays
      vi. qualifications
2. **Application form**
   a. An application form is the most commonly used method of collecting the information the firm will need about the applicant.
   b. It may include the following:
      i. Name
      ii. Address, telephone number
      iii. Date of birth
      iv. Working experience
      v. Education, qualifications
      vi. Interviews
      vii. They are the most frequently used method of selecting a potential employee.
3. **Testing**
   a. Testing provides information about the applicant's abilities. They include testing in the basic skills required to fill the position.
   b. This is normally a written examination.
   c. Successful applicants will then be required to undergo a complete medical examination to further satisfy their suitability for the vacant post.

## Compensation
1. **The most common payment systems are:**
   a. Piece rate
   b. Salary
   c. Wage
   d. Commission
   e. Performance-related pay
   f. Profit sharing
   g. Fringe benefits
   h. Pension funds
   i. Health insurance
2. **The human resources department has the responsibility of deciding which methods of financial reward should be applied in any given situation.**
3. **Human resources managers will give a ranking of each job to determine the compensation to be given and pay differentials between jobs. The actual level of pay may still be determined by bargaining with workers if there is no union representation, or through collective bargaining with workers if there is a trade union.**

## Training and development
1. **Development**
   a. Development of employees involves the future of employees.
   b. Development focuses on the development of a more general nature, e.g. problem solving and team working.
2. **Training**
   1. Training is the process that attempts to equip workers with the skills demanded by the job presently and in the future. This can be part of the following:
      a. Teambuilding
      b. Developing new skills
      c. Training for change
      d. Induction training.

2. Employees need training in the following areas:
   a. Established work practices and norms
   b. Use of tools and equipment
   c. Relations with (i) customers and (ii) suppliers
   d. Dealing with the firm's records
   e. The firm's health and safety regulations
   f. The firm's products.

3. A firm can use the following methods to train workers:
   a. Internal training
   b. External training
   c. A mixture of internal and external training
   d. Mentoring
   e. Personalised study programs.

4. Internal training vs. External training

| Internal training | External training |
|---|---|
| › It is valuable if the training needs are specific to the firm | This can be employed if<br>› there are only a few employees with the training need |
| › If trainers are internal, training will be specific to the firm, dealing with specific issues | › The training requirement is not specifically linked to the organisation |
| › If trainers are external, a wider set of issues will be covered, e.g. new ideas of accomplishing given tasks | › Trainees can meet workers from other firms and can exchange methods and ideas |
| | › It can increase motivation |
| | › It can increase productivity |

5. Benefits of training:
   a. It increases efficiency
   b. Reduces the cost to the firm in the long-run
   c. It increases the opportunity for promotion
   d. It increases motivation, therefore:
      i. Fewer accidents
      ii. Less labour turnover
      iii. Lower level of absenteeism
      iv. Fewer negative informal groups
      v. Reduces conflict

6. The two basic categories of training are:
   › On-the-job
   › Off-the-job

| On-the-job training | |
|---|---|
| **Advantages** | **Disadvantages** |
| › Cheaper as existing employees and equipment can be used | › The working environment may be noisy. Problems in communication |
| › Takes place in a more realistic surrounding | › It is not the best learning environment |
| › There is no problem for trainee to readjust from training to actual work | › The trainer may not have learnt best practices, therefore bad habits may be passed on to the trainee |
| › Learning can be put into practice immediately | › It is often not well organised. Trainees are expected to learn the job by doing it |
| › Trainer may know the job better than a full time trainer who may not have up-to-date knowledge | › They may be given boring and unpleasant jobs that workers often avoid |
| › It can be more relevant to the trainees as they are trained on the site | › Workers may not have acquired teaching skills |
| | › Trainees' interests are often ignored, especially when working under pressure |
| | › Trainees may be taken away from training to substitute for absent workers, or to assist when extra workers are needed in different areas of the firm |
| | › Untrained workers are a cost to the firm in terms of errors that they can make |

| Off-the-job training | |
|---|---|
| **Advantages** | **Disadvantages** |
| › Training is more valued as it is done by experts in the field | › The training environment may be too different from the working environment |
| › There is increased motivation | › Specialist trainers may have limited knowledge of techniques currently used in the firm |
| › Opportunities to meet staff from different firms – sharing of ideas | › It is usually more costly than on-the-job training |
| › Reduced stress | › It takes employees away from their work |
| › Training may take place in an environment conducive to learning | › Workers may fail to see the link between training and their work |
| › It is easier to give theoretical instructions | |
| › Training can me more concentrated | |

## Performance appraisal

1. Performance appraisal is the judgement of an employee's performance in his job.
2. It is a formal and systematic assessment by a superior of those for whom they responsible.
3. It must be fair.
4. Trainees must participate in appraisals.
5. Trainees must be able to say what they think about the appraisal.
6. It is formalised and conducted at prescribed times, e.g. 6 months or 1 year.
7. The objective of performance appraisal is to motivate employees to perform better.
8. Workers are involved in assessing and improving their own progress.
9. It attempts to quantify the skills needed for the job and set identifiable goals for employees.
10. Employees are required to sign the completed form along with their supervisor.
11. This may be followed by an interview that involves discussions on:
    a. Worker's performance
    b. Worker's strengths and weaknesses
    c. Need for training if necessary
    d. Scope for promotion
    e. Targets for the next year.

## Usefulness of performance appraisal

1. Performance appraisal increases worker morale, as good performance can be recognised
2. It motivates workers
3. It can indicate training needs, e.g. areas where performance needs improving
4. It acts as a basis for payments
5. It helps to communicate the firm's objectives
6. It provides information for decision-making
7. It reduces the element of subjectivity in assessing workers' performance
8. It improves worker performance
9. It helps the firm to establish future standards based on current performance

## Appraisal process

1. Objectives and procedures for the appraisal form
2. Completion of the appraisal form
3. Appraisal interview
4. Discussion of the future

## The personnel function includes performance appraisal

The objective here is to:

1. Improve present performance levels by identifying an individual's strengths and weaknesses.
2. Obtain information to determine pay levels.
3. Establish written performance records which can be used in the appraisal process.
4. Improve future performance by identifying individual potential for development and/ or promotion.

## Resistance to change

See section entitled 'Management of change' in this module.

## The importance of communication in the management process

1. **Motivating the workforce:** junior employees can have their views expressed. This will increase their staff worth and motivate them; e.g. quality circles, team working.
2. **Communication is the means by which the firm relates to society in general and potential consumers.** Effective communication through publicity can increase the firm's sales and profit margin.
3. **Effective internal communication can help to provide greater understanding of the differences in cultures and opinions within the firm.**
4. **Effective external communication is an essential part of achieving customer satisfaction.**

### Reasons for communication

> To give facts, e.g. profits increased by 50 per cent in the last six months.
> To give instructions, e.g. obey all health and safety regulations.
> In negotiating: we want next Saturday off.
> Asking for opinions: what venue should we use to hold our Christmas dinner?
> Influencing attitudes: if you become more qualified your salary will increase.

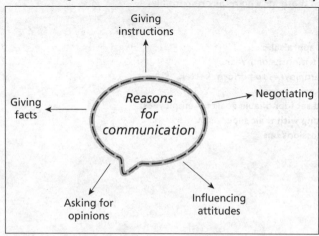

Reasons for communication

 QUICK TEST

1. State the role of human resources management, in a named firm.    **[10 marks]**
2. State the advantages of:
   (a) Internal recruitment.    **[10 marks]**
   (b) External recruitment.    **[10 marks]**
3. State the disadvantages of:
   (a) Internal recruitment.    **[10 marks]**
   (b) External recruitment.    **[10 marks]**
4. State the advantages and disadvantages of on-the-job training and off-the-job training.    **[20 marks]**
5. How is the effectiveness of the human resources department, determined?    **[15 marks]**

# MULTIPLE CHOICE QUESTIONS

**1.** The Hawthorne effect was 'discovered' by:
   a. John M. Keynes
   b. Elton Mayo from the Harvard Business School
   c. Abraham Maslow
   d. Douglas McGregor

**2.** Which one of the following theorists talks of Theory X and Theory Y workers?
   a. Douglas McGregor
   b. Frederick Herzberg
   c. Abraham Maslow
   d. Frederick Taylor

**3.** Autocratic leadership style is most effective in:
   I. The garment industry
   II. The military
   III. A situation where there is no time for consultation
   IV. A situation where there is time for consultation
   a. I only
   b. II, III
   c. I, II, III
   d. I, II, III, IV

**4.** In which of the following theories would Job Enlargement be classified:
   a. Maslow's Hierarchy of Needs
   b. Herzberg's two-factor Theory
   c. Taylor's Scientific Theory
   d. McGregor's Theory

**5.** The grapevine is an example of:
   a. Direct communication
   b. Informal communication
   c. Lateral communication
   d. Formal communication

**6.** The Articles of Association includes:
   I. The borrowing proceeds of the firm
   II. The rights of members at meetings
   III. The name and objective of the company
   IV. The powers of the directors
   a. I, IV
   b. I, III
   c. I, II, III
   d. I, II, III, IV

**7.** Which of the following are examples of non-financial incentives?
   I. Job enlargement
   II. Work study
   III. Job enrichment
   IV. Opportunities for promotion
   a. I, II
   b. I, II, III
   c. I, III, IV
   d. I, II, III, IV

**8.** Which of the following are the strategies to manage change?
   I. Avoidance
   II. Delegation
   III. Compromise
   IV. Confrontation
   a. I, II
   b. I, III, IV
   c. II, III
   d. I, II, III, IV

**9.** Communication is said to be effective when:
   a. What is said is understood in the way it was said, and there was feedback
   b. There is no noise in the environment
   c. The receiver receives the message
   d. The message is written

**10.** One advantage of the Matrix Organisational structure is:
   a. It allows for greater efficiency
   b. Clear functional responsibilities
   c. Each worker has only one supervisor
   d. There should be good communication and cooperation between functional departments

**11.** Matrix management can be described as:
   a. An approach to management in which teams of employees with appropriate skills are placed together to perform given tasks
   b. A management style aimed to foster growth in the firm
   c. A situation where all managers come together to formulate ideas
   d. A situation where management makes decisions without consulting workers

**12.** Human behaviour theorists believe that:
   a. Teamwork among members can lead to effective cooperation
   b. Workers satisfy their need through work
   c. Workers must be supervised at all times
   d. Workers must be treated fairly

**13.** Which of the following theorists believe that conflict is inevitable within a capitalist system?
   a. Elton Mayo
   b. Karl Marx
   c. Douglas McGregor
   d. Frederick Taylor

**14.** Who was the Scientific Management theorist?
   a. Frederick Taylor
   b. Elton Mayo
   c. Frederick Herzberg
   d. Max Weber

**15.** Who was the Classical Management theorist?
   a.   Maslow
   b.   McGregor
   c.   Fayol
   d.   Mayo

**16.** Which of the following theorists is associated with the Hawthorne Effect?
   a.   Elton Mayo
   b.   Frederick Taylor
   c.   Max Weber
   d.   Douglas McGregor

**17.** McGregor's Theory X assumes:
   I.    Workers have to be controlled
   II.   Workers avoid work
   III.  Workers concentrate on satisfying physiological and safety needs
   IV.  Workers want to satisfy social needs
   a.   I, IV
   b.   III, IV
   c.   I, II, III
   d.   I, II, III, IV

**18.** Delegation means:
   a.   Giving instruction to the upper levels in the hierarchy
   b.   Passing authority down the hierarchy
   c.   Passing authority and responsibility down the hierarchy
   d.   Having an autocratic form of management

# Unit 1
## Module 3

**Business finance and accounting**

# The need for capital

## Objectives
At the end of this section you will understand the:

1. Meaning of venture capital
2. Purpose of working capital in a firm
3. Importance of investment capital to a firm.

## Introduction
Capital is needed by a firm:

› **To purchase fixed assets.**
› **To cover daily expenses.**
› **For research and development.**
› **To enter new markets.**
› **For growth and expansion.**

## Start-up or venture capital
1. **This involves the sale of equity or a share in a business to another business or individuals.**
2. **The venture capitalist:**
    a. Buys an equity share in a firm with high potential growth.
    b. Often provides funds for businesses that are considered too risky for other investors.
    c. Invests in the business for a share in the business.
3. **Venture capital is needed:**
    a. In the start-up phase of the firm
    b. To expand the firm
    c. If the firm is experiencing financial problems.
4. **Advantages of venture capital:**
    a. The venture capitalist will provide advice to strengthen the firm
    b. The firm does not have to pay interest
    c. It will reduce the gearing of the firm
    d. Lower gearing makes it easier to raise finance.

## Working capital
1. **It is a firm's current assets minus current liabilities.**
2. **It is necessary for the daily operation of the firm.**
3. **It is money required to:**
    a. Buy materials and components
    b. Pay for the labour
    c. Pay for rent
    d. Pay for electricity
    e. Take advantage of trade discounts.
4. **The cost of holding too much cash includes:**
    a. Loss of purchasing power (inflation)
    b. Loss of interest
    c. Opportunity cost.
5. **Cost of holding too little cash includes:**
    a. Inability to meet creditors' demands
    b. Cannot take advantage of cash discounts
    c. May not be able to meet daily expenditures.

## Investment capital
This is the capital required by the firm to:

a. **Purchase its fixed assets, e.g. equipment, tools, buildings.**
b. **Replace worn out assets.**

---

 QUICK TEST

1. **Explain why a firm would need start-up/venture capital.**            [10 marks]
2. **Explain the importance of working capital for a named firm.**        [10 marks]
3. **Discuss the role of investment capital for a named firm.**           [10 marks]

# Sources of finance

## Objectives

At the end of this section, you will know the:

1. Difference between:
   a. Equity financing, and
   b. Debt financing.
2. Different forms of equity financing.
3. Different forms of debt financing.

### Equity versus debt

#### i. Equity

› Equity is money received from the sales of shares.
› It also consists of any reserves and profits reinvested into the business.
› Holders of equity capital receive dividends on their investment.
› Dividends may vary according to the firm's profitability.
› Equity is provided by the risk takers of the firm.
› Risk takers have some decision-making powers, and can vote.

#### ii. Debt finance

› Debt finance is provided by creditors, e.g. banks.
› A fixed rate of interest is charged to be paid at a specific time.
› A penalty is charged for delayed payment.
› Debenture holders contribute to debt financing.
› Debenture holders have no voting rights and no decision-making powers.

### Forms of equity: capital and shares

#### i. Capital

› Is profits retained by the firm after taxation.
› Is a major source of finance for a firm that wants to invest in fixed assets.
› May be more cost-effective than a bank loan.

#### ii. Shares

› Provide finance for the firm.
› Shareholders become part-owner of the firm.
› Ordinary shareholders have voting rights.
› There is no guaranteed dividend for ordinary shareholders.
› Ordinary shareholders may not be paid if the firm makes no profit.
› Preference shareholders receive a fixed rate of return/dividends.
› Preference shareholders receive dividends before ordinary shareholders.
› Some preference shares are cumulative, i.e. dividends can accumulate from one year to the next.

### Forms of debt: debentures and bonds

#### i. Debentures

› Debentures are loan capital.
› Debenture holders do not have voting rights at annual general meetings.
› Rate of intervals on debentures are fixed
› Debenture holders can sell debentures to a third-party.
› Debentures are long-term debt.
› A debenture is a suitable form of finance for a well-established business with a healthy balance sheet.

#### ii. Bonds

› Holders of bonds receive a fixed rate of interest
› They have no voting rights
› If the firm cannot make payments on maturity of the bond, the firm's assets can be sold to make the necessary payments

 QUICK TEST

1. State and explain the different types of shares a firm can issue. [10 marks]
2. Explain the importance of debentures and bonds to a firm. [10 marks]
3. Explain the difference between equity financing and debt financing. [10 marks]

# Criteria for seeking finance

## Objectives
At the end of this section, you will know:
1. Short-term sources of finance.
2. Long-term sources of finance.
3. The advantages and disadvantages of various forms of short-term and long-term financing.

## Sources of short-term finance
### i. Bank overdraft
› The firm can 'overdraw' its account by writing cheques to a greater value than the balance in the account, but there is a limit.
› If necessary, the overdraft can be increased for a short period.
› Rate of interest is high.

### ii. Trade credit
› The firm can buy goods on credit.
› The problem for the firm is that it may not be able to benefit from cash discounts.

### iii. Debt factors
› Firms can sell debts to a debt factor and obtain immediate cash.

## Sources of long-term finance
### i. Commercial banks
› Provide long-term investment or development loans.
› Rate of interest is the market level.
› Requirement for loan:
  o Business plan
  o Collateral
  o Cash flow forecast
  o Recent business accounts.

### ii. Development banks
› They are specialist institutions; they lend to small or medium-sized businesses.
› They lend to businesses that cannot obtain funding from commercial banks.
› Rate of interest is lower than commercial banks.
› Objectives may be non-profit making.

### iii. Venture capital funds
› Venture capitalists provide finance for a firm in return for shares or part-ownership of the business.
› They receive dividends from profits.
› Venture capital can be used for growth and expansion of the company.

### iv. Small business associations
› Provide loans for small businesses.
› Rate of interest is low.
› Provide advice for small businesses.

### v. Development funds
› Fund aid: helps small firms to grow by providing capital and advice.
› Small Business Development Company of Trinidad and Tobago: offers loans and advice.
› Business Development Company: offers financial aid and advice to larger enterprises.

### vi. Family
› Provide start-up funding or expansion of micro or small business.
› Rate of interest is low.
› Amount of loan can be limited.
› There is normally a loss of control.

## Short-term versus long-term finance
### i. Financial obligations
A firm may need finance to cover its financial obligations. The firm's manager must decide:

› How much finance is needed.
› If finance can be obtained internally.

› **If it is needed to cover capital or revenue expenditure.**
› **Whether it should use short-term or long-term financing.**

## ii. Long-term capital

This is needed for capital expenditure.

## iii. Short-term capital

This is used to finance, for example, wages or the purchase of stock.

## iv. Decision to take short-term or long-term finance

This depends on the purpose and use of the finance. The following are some factors to consider:

› **The purpose of raising the finance, that is, if it is for short-term expenditure, e.g. to pay debtors, then short-term finance is needed.**
› **If it is to finance long-term expansion plans, then long-term financing is needed.**
› **The manager's attitude to risk: if managers want to avoid too much risk, then they would issue shares.**
› **The current and expected levels of interest rates: if interest rates are expected to rise in the future, then short-term financing will be used.**

---

## QUICK TEST

| | | |
|---|---|---|
| 1. | State and explain the role of trade creditors in providing finance for a firm. | [10 marks] |
| 2. | What are the advantages of obtaining short-term finance from commercial banks? | [10 marks] |
| 3. | State the disadvantages of obtaining short-term finance from commercial banks. | [10 marks] |
| 4. | List the various agencies that provide long-term financing to a firm. | [10 marks] |
| 5. | When would a firm use short-term financing? And long-term financing? | [10 marks] |

# Money and capital markets and international financial institutions

## Objectives

At the end of this section, you will know the:

1. International financial institutions that operate in the Caribbean.
2. Aims and objectives of each financial institution.

## Roles of regional and international financial institutions

### i. Caribbean Development Bank (CDB)

1. **Functions of the CDB are to:**
   o Assist regional members in coordinating development programs to help better the utilisation of their resources.
   o Mobilise within and outside the region, additional financial resources.
   o Finance projects and programs that contribute to the development of the region.
   o Undertake or commission surveys or by assisting in the identification of proposals in order to provide appropriate technical assistance.
   o Encourage and stimulate capital market development within the region.

2. **Role of the CDB is to:**
   o Contribute in the growth and development of the Caribbean.
   o Promote economic cooperation among Caribbean states.
   o Provide loans to Caribbean governments at a lower rate of interest than banks; for example; contribution of highways.

### ii. International Monetary Fund (IMF)

Aims of the IMF are to:

› **Promote international cooperation.**
› **Facilitate world trade growth.**
› **Provide finance to countries facing a balance of payments problem.**
› **Promote high levels of employment.**
› **Eliminate exchange restrictions.**
› **Promote exchange stability, that is, an orderly exchange among its members.**
› **Establish a multinational system.**
› **Provide advice to governments on economic policy issues.**
› **Provide training for government staff.**

### iii. World Bank

› **This bank was created to guarantee loans for development projects that would be provided by its member governments.**
› **Its share capital is structured in such a way that any risk incurred would be shared by all member governments.**
› **The bank mainly relies on the world's capital markets for the bulk of its financial resources.**
› **Provides financial assistance to countries.**
› **Provides technical assistance.**
› **It is not aimed at making a profit.**
› **Objective is to reduce poverty and improve the standard of living.**
› **The International Bank for Reconstruction and Development (IBRD) focuses on middle-income countries and credit-worthy poor countries.**
› **The Inter-Development Association (IDA) is concerned mainly with the poorest countries in the world.**
› **They provide low interest loans, internet free credit and grants to developing countries for environmental projects, education, health and infrastructure.**
› **The bank provides technical and managerial advice to local workers, government staff and businesses to ensure that workers in the domestic economy can undertake part of the project.**
› **Conducts feasibility study to determine the benefit of each project to the economy.**

### iv. Inter-American Development Bank (IADB)

› **Established to service the needs of the independent countries of North and South America and the Caribbean.**
› **Provides finances for development.**

## Stock exchange

All stock exchanges have the following objectives:

› **Provide facilities for the trade in shares and bonds.**
› **Ensure that the stock market and its members operate at the highest standards possible.**
› **Conduct research and disseminate relevant information.**
› **Insist on the minimum requirements for the listing of a company's shares on the market to give investors' confidence in the standing and trading record of companies.**
› **Require listed companies to provide regular audited accounts to the exchange.**
› **Enable mergers and takeovers to take place smoothly.**
› **Provide a means of protection for shareholders (they have rules and regulations).**
› **Could reflect the state of the economy.**
› **Provide a market where companies can sell shares; this is their main function.**
› **Enable the firm to obtain finance by selling shares.**

---

 QUICK TEST

1. **Explain the role of the IMF in developing countries.**     [10 marks]
2. **Explain the role of the Stock Exchange.**     [10 marks]

# The need for accounting information

## Objectives

At the end of this section, you will:

1. Understand the concept of accounting
2. Know the uses of accounting information to the various stakeholders

## Definition of accounting

It is the systematic recording of financial information of a business over a given time period. The main accounts are: profit and loss account, balance sheet and cash flow statements.

## Users of accounting information

i. **Financial institutions:** to judge the level of risk of an investment in relation to the expected possible returns.

ii. **Suppliers:** they will look at financial accounts to determine the firm's ability to pay; this would help them to decide how much credit to give and the time frame.

iii. **Managers (i.e. all managers; junior, middle, top):** junior and middle managers use it to see areas of inefficiency and to help them stay within budgets; senior managers need it to assist them in decision-making for medium- and long-term planning and to set targets for the firm to:
   o Measure the performance of the firm
   o Compare targets with actual performance.

iv. **Investors:** financial data that is publicly available assists investors to compare different firms' financial status and act as a guide to them when making investment choices:
   o Measure the performance of the firm.
   o Determine what share of the profit the investors will receive.
   o Decide whether to keep their investment in the given firm or remove all or some of it.
   o Anticipate the potential for future growth.
   o Make comparisons with other firms before deciding where to invest.

v. **Board of directors:** they use financial information to explain to shareholders the financial state of the firm and to analyse the past decision and to identify areas of strength, weakness and inefficiency.

vi. **Owners:** to establish if the business is being well managed. They want to know the profitability of the venture, financial stability and the return on their investment.

vii. **The Government and tax authorities** use financial information to:
   o Calculate the level of taxes to be paid.
   o Understand the possible potential to create more employment.
   o Understand how viable the firm is.
   o Ensure the firm is operating according to the established accounting regulations.

viii. **Customers:** to determine if there will be future suppliers of the firm's output and to decide if there will be after-sales-services.

ix. **Local community** uses accounting information to determine:
   o If the business is profitable.
   o The survival of the firm.
   o If the firm will expand.

x. **Workforce** uses accounting information to:
   o Determine if their jobs are secure.
   o Compare wages of different categories of workers.
   o Determine if the firm is likely to grow.
   o Determine if the firm can pay wages and salaries.

 QUICK TEST

1. **Explain the importance of accounting information to:**
   a. Managers
   b. Investors
   c. Suppliers
   d. Financial institutions. **[20 marks]**

# Components of financial statements

## Objectives

At the end of this section, you will:

1. **Explain the components of financial statements.**
2. **Know the format and calculations of the components of financial statements.**

## (a) Components of financial statements

### i. Income statement:

**(COMPANY NAME)**
Income Statement
For the year ending _____

| | $ | $ |
|---|---|---|
| Sales Revenue | | 1,000 |
| *Less:* Cost of Sales: | | |
| Opening Stock | 150 | |
| *Add:* Purchases | 350 | |
| | 500 | |
| *Less:* Closing Stock | (50) | |
| Cost of Sales | | (450) |
| Gross Profit / (Loss) | | 550 |
| *Less:* Expenses: | | |
| Administration | 100 | |
| Selling and Distribution | 75 | |
| Financial | 75 | |
| Total Expenses | | (250) |
| Net Profit / (Loss) | | 300 |

## ii. Balance sheet

**(COMPANY NAME)**
**Balance sheet**
**As at _____**

| | $ | $ | $ |
|---|---|---|---|
| **Fixed Assets:** | | | |
| Premises | | 50,000 | |
| Plant Equipment | 20,000 | | |
| Less: Accumulated Depreciation | (5,000) | 15,000 | |
| Total Fixed Assets | | | 65,000 |
| **Current Assets:** | | | |
| Stock | 50 | | |
| Debtors | 300 | | |
| Bank | 500 | | |
| Cash | 200 | | |
| | | 1,050 | |
| *Less:* **Current Liabilities:** | | | |
| Creditors | 250 | | |
| Provision for tax | 100 | | |
| Overdraft | 50 | | |
| | | (400) | |
| Working Capital | | | 650 |
| | | | |
| *Less:* **Long Term Liabilities:** | | | (300) |
| Net Assets | | | **65,350** |
| **Equity** | | | |
| Shareholders' Funds: | | | |
| Share Issues | | 45,000 | |
| Share Premium | | 15,000 | |
| Reserves | | 5,350 | |
| | | | **65,350** |

> The balance sheet is a financial statement recording the assets and liabilities of a firm at the end of an accounting period.
> By recording assets and liabilities, the balance sheet will set out ways by which the firm can raise capital.
> It also shows the uses to which the capital has been put.
> It provides information to calculate ratio analysis.
> It records the net wealth of firms at a specific time.

## iii. Cash flow statements

1. The purpose of cash flow statements are:
   o To plan when to finance major expenditure.
   o To plan how to finance major expenditure.
   o To ensure that liquid assets are available to meet payments.
   o To identify periods when there is a cash surplus.
   o When there is a cash surplus that can be used for other purposes to assure leaders that cash borrowed/ loans can be repaid.
   o Can indicate to the firm when cash outflows will exceed cash inflows.
2. The simple cash flow forecast has three main headings:
   a. Receipts: will include expected income received by the firm.
   b. Payments: will include expected expenditure by the firm, e.g. payment of instalments.
   c. Running balance: the expected bank balance at the beginning and the end of each month.

**Name of Company**
**Cash Flow Forecast Statement**
**for period ending** _____

| | Jan | Feb | Mar | Apr | May | June |
|---|---|---|---|---|---|---|
| | $ | $ | $ | $ | $ | $ |
| **Receipts:** | | | | | | |
| 1 Sales Cash | 1,000 | 1,100 | 1,200 | 1,300 | 1,000 | 1,200 |
| 2 Sales Credit | 400 | 450 | 500 | 450 | 500 | 650 |
| 3 Total cash in (Add Rows 1 & 2) | 1,400 | 1,550 | 1,700 | 1,750 | 1,500 | 1,850 |
| | | | | | | |
| **Payments:** | | | | | | |
| 4 Supplies | 350 | 388 | 425 | 400 | 375 | 500 |
| 5 Wages | 140 | 155 | 170 | 175 | 150 | 185 |
| 6 Drawings | 50 | 55 | 60 | 65 | 50 | 60 |
| 7 Electricity | 100 | 100 | 100 | 100 | 100 | 100 |
| 8 Heating | 25 | 25 | 25 | 25 | 25 | 25 |
| 9 Rates | 50 | 50 | 50 | 50 | 50 | 50 |
| 10 Mortgage Payment | 200 | 200 | 200 | 200 | 200 | 200 |
| 11 Interest on Loan | 50 | 50 | 50 | 50 | 50 | 50 |
| 12 Total Cash Out (Add Rows 4 to 11) | (965) | (1,023) | (1,080) | (1,065) | (1,000) | (1,170) |
| | | | | | | |
| 13 Net Cash Flow (Row 3 minus Row 12) | 435 | 528 | 620 | 685 | 500 | 680 |
| 14 Opening Bank Balance | 200 | 635 | 1,163 | 1,783 | 2,468 | 2,968 |
| 15 Closing Bank Balance (Add Rows 13 & 14) | 635 | 1,163 | 1,783 | 2,468 | 2,968 | 3,648 |

Simple format cash flow forecast

**Name of Company**
**Cash Flow Statement**
**for period ending** _____

| | | |
|---|---|---|
| Cash Flows from Operating Activities: | | |
| Earnings before Interest and Taxes (EBIT) | 1,000 | |
| Depreciation Expense | 100 | |
| Loss on Sale of Equipment | 50 | |
| Gain on Sale of Land | (150) | |
| (Increase)/Decrease in Debtors | (25) | |
| (Increase)/Decrease in Prepayments | 15 | |
| Increase/ (Decrease) in Creditors | 50 | |
| Net Cash Flow from Operating Actvivities | | 940 |
| | | |
| Cash Flow from Investing Activities: | | |
| Sale of Equipment | 20 | |
| Sale of Land | 250 | |
| Purchase of Equipment | (300) | |
| Net Cash Flow from Investing Activities | | (30) |
| | | |
| Cash Flows from Financing Activities: | | |
| Payment of Dividends | (15) | |
| Issue of Shares | 150 | |
| Payment of Bond | (100) | |
| Net Cash Flow from Financing Activities | | 35 |
| Net Change in Cash | | 945 |
| Beginning Cash Balance | | 200 |
| Ending Cash Balance | | 1,145 |

Alternate (detailed) format: cash flow statement using the indirect method

# Financial statement analysis

## Objectives

At the end of this section, you will know the:

1. **Uses of accounting ratios.**
2. **Disadvantages of using ratio analysis in decision-making.**
3. **Advantages of using ratio analysis in decision-making.**
4. **Ratios listed below and how to calculate them:**
   a. Liquidity ratios
   b. Profitability ratios
   c. Efficiency ratios
   d. Gearing ratios
   e. Shareholder ratios.

## Use of ratio analysis

1. **Ratio analysis is a technique for analysing a business's financial performance by comparing one piece of accounting information with another. Ratios can be used to access the profitability, efficiency and solvency of the firm over a period of time.**
2. **Some of its uses are:**
   o To identify possible problems before they occur.
   o To assess the performance of the firm.
   o In decision-making by various stakeholders.
   o To establish the interrelationship between variables.
   o To summarise data.
   o In forecasting and planning.
   o To analyse:
     ▪ Profitability of the firm
     ▪ Liquidity of the firm
     ▪ Efficiency of the firm.
3. **Users of accounting ratios:**
   Ratios can be used by:
   o Managers: to maintain the performance of the business.
   o Suppliers: to determine whether to offer credit, and to assess the possibility of receiving payment.
   o Employers: to anticipate pay increases.
   o Competitors: to benchmark their performance against a given firm.
   o Employees and Trade Unions.
   o Bank managers.
   o Researchers.
   o Press.
   o Inland Revenue Department.
   o Debtors and creditors.
   o Pressure groups.

## Advantages of ratio analysis

› **Gives an in-depth interpretation of data.**
› **Identifies trends.**
› **Measures the different aspects of the firm's performance.**
› **Shows the value of a firm.**
› **Shows the firm's efficiency.**
› **Shows the firm's profitability.**
› **Ratios provide a framework for identifying problems rather than adding anything to decision-making.**

## Limitations of ratio analysis

› **Accounting information is not precise.**
› **Inter-firm comparisons are only valid if the firms use the same method in calculating depreciation and stock valuation.**

> Comparisons over time are difficult because of inflation and changes in the external environment; for example, changes in exchange rate, changes in interest rates, changes in taxation, or changes in industrial policy, may cause the profitability ratio to appear to be healthy, but in fact this may not be the case. Efficiency did not improve
> Ratios are only part of the equation for understanding a firm's performance. Other factors must be considered. For example, non-quantitative factors, such as labour relations, quality of the workforce and goodwill.
> Published accounts are historic. Ratios based on published accounts may not be valid today.
> Some ratios can be calculated using different formulae; when comparisons are made it is important to use the same formula.
> Ratios are only concerned with accounting items that have a number value. Non-numerical values are now important in assessing a firm's performance; for example, environmental factors.
> Ratio results can be affected when different firms uses different depreciation methods. This can lead to different capital employed figures. This can affect certain ratio results.
> Trend analysis needs to take into account factors in the external environment (such as, inflation) that can affect ratio results.
> A firm must use more than one ratio in order to make a more accurate comparison with other firms, or over different time periods.
> Ratios are distorted by short-term fluctuations and by their timing.
> Ratios indicate a problem but they do not give a solution.
> No account is taken of changes in strategy or management over a period of time.
> No account is taken of external influences; for example, trade cycle or a competitor's action.

## Calculation and interpretation of types of ratios

### i. Liquidity ratios
> These measure the extent to which a firm can meet its immediate financial obligations.
> It is the proportion of assets that can be easily converted into cash.
> A firm is considered 'liquid' if it holds a high proportion of liquid assets, e.g. cash and debtors.
> However, holding too many liquid assets has an opportunity cost attached to it.
> A firm therefore has to establish a balance between operating with few liquid assets against operating with more capital investments.
> These ratios include:
  o Current ratio
  o Acid test ratio

### The current ratio
> As a general rule, the current ratio should be between 1.5 and 2. This is a rough guide.
> If the ratio is too low, the firm will have problems in repaying its debts.
> If the ratio is greater than 2, it may be that the firm is holding excess current assets, e.g. bank balances or excess stocks.
> If it is holding excess stocks, then the firm may have to sell it off at a discounted rate to meet its current liabilities.
> The acid test ratio gives a better indication of the firm's liquidity.

Formula:

$$\text{Current ratio} = \frac{\text{Current assets}}{\text{Current liabilities}}$$

### Acid test (or quick) ratio
> As a general rule, the acid test (or quick) ratio should equal 1.
> If the cash held by the firm and cash owed to the firm is equal to the firm's current liabilities, the firm will be able to meet its financial liabilities.
> The firms, therefore, will not have to sell off its stocks at a reduced price.
> A low acid test ratio does not imply financial problems for the firm in the long run, if the firm has a seasonal demand for its output. For example, expenditure would be greater than revenue for toy stores in November; however, by the end of December (Christmas holidays), the financial position would improve.

Formula:

$$\text{Acid test (quick) ratio} = \frac{(\text{cash} + \text{debtors}) \text{ or } (\text{current assets} - \text{stock})}{\text{current liabilities}}$$

## ii. Profitability ratios

Profitability ratios relate profits to sales and assets

They include:

> **Gross profit margin**
> **Gross profit mark-up**
> **Return on capital employed (ROCE)**
> **Net profit margin.**

## Gross profit margin

This ratio shows the percentage profit from sales that is available to cover the cost of overheads. Most firms will require a gross profit of at least 20 per cent.

If the ratio is falling, it could be because:

> **The increase in cost is not passed on to customers.**
> **Fraudulent activity has taken place.**
> **Stocks have been lost.**
> **The firm wants to extend its market share so prices are kept down.**

Formula:

$$\text{Gross profit margin} = \frac{\text{Gross profit} \times 100}{\text{Sales}}$$

The amount of gross profit percentage made on consumer durables is higher than that made on food items.

## Gross profit mark-up

Mark-up is the amount of profit added to cost of goods sold. A low mark-up might indicate that the firm wants to increase gross profit by gaining increased sales.

Formula:

$$\text{Gross profit mark-up} = \frac{\text{Gross profit} \times 100}{\text{Cost of sales}}$$

## Return on capital employed (ROCE)

> **It measures the operational efficiency of the business in using its capital to generate profits.**
> **If ROCE is lower than interest rates, it would be wise for the firm to put the money in the bank.**
> **To assess the ROCE figure for a firm, it should be compared to:**
>   1. The ROCE of other companies
>   2. The current rate of interest
>   3. The business ROCE figure for previous years.

Formula:

$$\text{ROCE} = \frac{\text{Net profit before interest and tax} \times 100}{\text{Total capital employed}}$$

## Net profit margin

It measures the relationship between the net profit (that is, the profit made after all other expenses have been deducted and the level of turnover or sales is made. Interest is excluded because it shows the operational efficiency of the business.

Formula:

$$\text{Net profit margin} = \frac{\text{Net profit (Earnings before interest and tax)} \times 100}{\text{Sales revenue}}$$

## iii. Efficiency/Activity ratios

Efficiency ratios indicate how efficient a firm has been.
These include:

> **Stock turnover ratio**
> **Average trade debtor collection period or debtor days**
> **Average trade creditor payment period or creditor days.**

## Stock turnover ratio

> **A high stock turnover indicates the firm is efficient.**
> **Stock turnover will vary according to the nature of business.**

> Firms supplying high-priced goods will turnover stocks more slowly.
> Firms supplying low-priced goods will turnover more rapidly.

Formula:

$$\text{Stock turnover} = \frac{\text{Cost of sales for period}}{\text{Average stock}}$$

$$\text{Where average stock} = \frac{(\text{Opening stock} + \text{closing stock})}{2}$$

## Average trade debtor collection period or debtor days

> This ratio shows the average time taken by a firm to collect its debts.
> If debtors are taking a long time to pay their debts, the firm could face problems receiving future payments from debtors.
> Different industries allow different terms for debtors to make payments, e.g. 30, 60 or 90 days.
> The debt collection period should be compared against the time the firm sets for payment.
> However, the shorter the debt collection period, the better.

Formula:

$$\text{Debt collection period} = \frac{\text{Average trade debtors} \times 365}{\text{Total credit sales}}$$

## Average trade creditor payment period or creditor days

> This shows the average length of time taken by the firm to pay its own debts.
> If it is rising, it would indicate difficulties for the firm in paying its debts.

Formula:

$$\text{Credit payment period} = \frac{\text{Average trade debtors} \times 365}{\text{Total credit purchases}}$$

## iv. Gearing ratio

> The gearing ratio establishes the balance between loan and share capital
> To establish the ability of a firm to meet its interest payments, the following formula is used.

Formula:

$$\text{Gearing ratio} = \frac{\text{Debt}}{\text{Capital employed}} \times 100$$

Where, Debt = Long-term debts

Capital employed = Fixed assets + current assets − current liabilities

## v. Investors/shareholder ratios

These ratios enable the investor to make an assessment on the return of the investment made. Ratios include:

> Dividend yield
> Earnings per share

## Dividend yield

> The dividend on a share is expressed as a percentage of its market share.
> This may not be useful to shareholders who have paid more than the nominal price of the share.

Formula:

$$\text{Dividend yield} = \frac{\text{Declared dividend per share}}{\text{Market share price}} \times 100$$

## Earnings per share (EPS)

> The EPS is found by dividing the possible profits available for distribution by the number of shares.
> It may be lower than the dividend per share.
> The reason being that some of the money available for distribution is kept as retained profits.

Formula:

$$\text{EPS} = \frac{\text{Profits available for ordinary shareholders}}{\text{Number of shares}}$$

QUICK TEST

1. **Discuss the importance of accounting ratios to the firm's various stakeholders.**          **[15 marks]**
2. **Discuss why ratio analysis must be used with caution.**          **[15 marks]**
3. **Explain:**
    a.   The importance of liquidity ratios to a firm.          **[10 marks]**
    b.   What a firm can to do increase liquidity.          **[15 marks]**
4. **What are the consequences for a firm that is too liquid?**          **[10 marks]**

# Budgets and budgetary control

## Objectives

At the end of this section, you will:

1. **Know the following budgets' composition and uses:**
   a. Cash budget
   b. Sales budget
   c. Production budget
   d. Material budget
   e. Purchases budget
   f. Labour budget
2. **Know the importance of setting budgets in a firm.**
3. **Know the limitations of setting budgets.**

## Budgets

A budget is a quantifiable plan for a defined period of time; for example, quarterly materials budget. Budgets are useful for the following:

1. **Setting targets, i.e. what has to be achieved.**
2. **Communication of targets, i.e. telling people what has to be done.**
3. **Coordination to ensure everyone is working together and that resources are properly allocated.**
4. **Controlling use of resources.**
5. **Monitoring performance.**
6. **Allocating responsibilities, i.e. deciding who is doing what.**

### Types of budgets

### i. Cash budget

› **To manage the cash flow, a firm will construct a cash budget.**
› **It summarises anticipated cash receipts and payments over the budgeted period.**
› **Cash receipts are based on the sales budget adjusted to account for the expected credit period allowed to debtors.**
› **It includes budgeted sales of fixed assets or expected capital issues.**
› **It includes outflow of cash for: payments of labour, materials and other expenses.**
› **Capital expenditure is also added.**
   Format:
   Cash inflow → [credit sales + cash sales + other inflows]
   *Less:*
   Cash outflow → [purchases + wages + utilities + rent + insurance + dividends]
   =
   Net cash flow for the period
   *Add:*
   Opening cash → [closing balance of previous year]
   =
   Closing cash

### ii. Sales budget

› **Sales units and the value are calculated on information:**
   o From past sales.
   o Current market research.
   o From an estimate of the competition.

### iii. Production budget

› **A production budget is based on the sales budget.**
› **It includes budgeted changes in stock.**
› **The production budget includes cost of materials, labour and machinery through the following budgets:**
   o Materials: material usage budget
   o Labour: wages budget
   o Machine operating budget: machine utilisation budget.

## Importance of budgeting

> Budgets provide targets to be met. They give a sense of direction.
> They help to coordinate the various departments in the firm.
> They improve communication.
> They ensure that capital is used for the established planned level of activity.
> Budgeting controls income and expenditure.
> It allows the firm to review its operations, allowing time for corrective action.
> It helps in monitoring performance.
> It can motivate middle management by giving them freedom within the budget.
> It allocates responsibility to the departmental managers.

## Usefulness and limitations of budgeting

| Usefulness of budgeting | Limitations of budgeting |
| --- | --- |
| > It improves communication | > If budgets are too flexible the firm can suffer |
| > It controls expenditure | > The budget can prove to be ineffective if the actual business results are different from the budgeted ones |
| > It fosters coordination | > If key personnel in the firm are not involved in the preparation of the budget, it may cause resentment |
| > Scarce resources are used in the most efficient way | > Uses up the firm's scarce resources |
| > Performance can be measured against targets | > Value depends on the quality of information gathered |
| > It motivates management | > Management can become too dependent on the budget and neglect the process of management |
| > Responsibilities are clarified | |

## Budgetary control

> The process of converting plans into budgets is called budgeting.
> The process of checking on whether budgets are being met is budgetary control.
> Budgetary control is the establishment of budgets and the continuous comparison of actual and budgeted results in order to determine variances from the plan and to provide a basis for revision of the objective. It involves:
  1. Preparation of the firm's plans
  2. Comparing the plans with actual results
  3. Analysing variances: to determine unfavourable or favourable variance (see 'Variance analysis' below)
> The whole budgeting control process consists of mainly revenue and capital budgets, based on functional activities, plus a master budget which summarises all of them.

## Advantages of budgetary control

1. Budgetary control prevents or reduces wasting of resources.
2. It regulates expenditure to fit into the firm's income.
3. It ensures that finance is readily available.
4. It encourages management to adopt systematic reporting procedures.
5. It encourages cooperation and coordination.
6. It assigns responsibility to specific individuals and departments and, by monitoring actual performances, helps to identify underachievement.
7. It forces management to use machines and labour efficiently.
8. It encourages management to consider the cost of idle resources.

## Variance analysis

> A variance represents the difference between expected cost or budgeted costs, revenue and profits and the actual figures.
> Variance is favourable if costs are lower than anticipated, or revenue and profits are higher than anticipated.
> Variance is adverse when costs are higher than budgeted or revenue or profits are lower than forecast.

## Causes of variances

Causes of variance include the following:

› **Storage and wastage of material**
› **Material cost (cheaper or more expensive)**
› **Efficiency changes**
› **Morale and efficiency of staff**
› **Wages (changes)**
› **Quality of material.**

---

 QUICK TEST

1. **Explain the usefulness of budgeting.** [15 marks]
2. **Explain the limitations of budgeting.** [15 marks]
3. **Explain what is meant by budgetary control.** [8 marks]

# Investment appraisal

## Objectives

At the end of this section, you will:

1. **Understand why firms would need investment**
2. **Know the advantages and disadvantages of various investment appraisal techniques.**

### Need for investment appraisal

> Investment appraisal techniques make comparisons between the likely cost of a proposal project and the expected returns to be gained from the investment.
> It can be used to help decision-makers decide whether to undertake a particular investment.

### Analytical methods of appraisal

i. Payback period
ii. Average rate of return (ARR)
iii. Net present value (NPV)

### Payback period

This technique evaluates individual investment projects in terms of the time taken to recover the original outlay of finances.

| | Cash Flows | |
|---|---|---|
| | Project A ($) | Project B ($) |
| **Initial Investment** | (50,000) | (20,000) |
| Cash flow Year 1 | 16,000 | 12,000 |
| Cash flow Year 2 | 16,000 | 8,000 |
| Cash flow Year 3 | 18,000 | 4,000 |
| Cash flow Year 4 | 18,000 | 2,000 |

The Payback for Project A is 3 years.
The Payback for Project B is 2 years.

| Advantages of Payback | Disadvantages of Payback |
|---|---|
| > Easy to calculate | > Excludes payments made after Payback |
| > Simple to understand | > Does not calculate profit |
| > Improves cash flow | > Ignores timing of payments |

### Average rate of return (ARR)

Average rate of return measures the net return each year as a percentage of the initial cost of the investment.
Formula:

$$ARR = \frac{\text{Net return (profit) per annum}}{\text{Capital outlay cost}} \times 100$$

| Advantages of ARR | Disadvantages of ARR |
|---|---|
| > It measures the profit achieved on projects | > It does not take into account the effect of time on the value of money |
| > A range of products can be compared | > It calculates average profits |
| > It is easy to identify the opportunity cost of the project | |

## Net present value (NPV)

> **Net present value is the value of income generated by an investment minus its cost.**
> **It is expressed in terms of its current (present) value.**
> **Future earnings are converted into present-day values through a discounting process.**
> **The expected rate of interest is used to calculate and bring future earnings to present-day worth.**
> **The longer the time period under consideration, the less the value of investment in current day terms.**

| Advantages of NPV | Disadvantages of NPV |
|---|---|
| › It allows for better quality investment decision to be made | › It is complex to calculate |
| › It takes into account cash inflows and outflows for the duration of the project | › It is easily misunderstood |
| › It allows firms to compare the worth of two or more projects, where income is received at different times | › Choosing the discounted rate is difficult especially for long-term projects |
| | › It is based on expectation |

## QUICK TEST

1. With the aid of an example, discuss the payback period.  [15 marks]
2. What are the advantages of the average rate of return (ARR) investment technique over the net present value (NPV) technique?  [15 marks]

# MULTIPLE CHOICE QUESTIONS

**1.** A Cash Flow forecast is important:
   a. It is used by the Board of Inland Revenue
   b. As it will tell how profitable a firm is
   c. It helps with the firm's financial planning
   d. It allows the firm to borrow money

**2.** Liquid Assets can be described as:
   a. Assets which change with time
   b. Items owned by a firm that can easily and quickly converted into cash
   c. Assets no longer needed by the firm
   d. Assets that the firm will hold for future investment

**3.** Which of the following BEST defines a debenture?
   a. A special type of long-term loan to be repaid at a future date
   b. A special type of short-term loan
   c. Funding the firm will receive from government
   d. The right to vote at Annual General Meetings

**4.** The Cash Flow Statement of a company shows:
   a. How the cash position of the company has changed over a period of time
   b. A forecast of cash inflows and outflows for the next year
   c. Where the outflows of company's funds went
   d. The source of income for the year

**5.** Factoring can be described as:
   a. The purchase of a new factory
   b. The cost of a factor of production
   c. The selling of debts to a debt factor in exchange for immediate liquidity
   d. Combining the factors of production to produce a given output

**6.** Limited liability means that:
   a. Shareholders can lose only what they originally invested in the firm, if the firm goes bankrupt
   b. The powers of the directors are limited by the Memorandum of Association
   c. There is a limit to the number of shareholders in the firm
   d. There is a limit to the amount of money a firm can borrow

**7.** Venture Capital can be BEST described as:
   a. The provision of long-term finance in exchange for shares in the firm
   b. A form of savings for a firm
   c. Dividends given to shareholders
   d. A subsidy given by the government to the firm

**8.** Working Capital can be defined as:
   a. The amount of Capital the firm has retained
   b. The machinery a firm has to work with
   c. A firm's current assets less its current liabilities
   d. The amount of money a firm borrows

**9.** 'Shareholder's Funds' are referred to as:
   a. Loans
   b. Equity
   c. Investment
   d. Working Capital

**10.** Which of the following is NOT an Investment Appraisal technique?
   a. Payback Period
   b. Cost/Benefit Analysis
   c. Average Rate of Return
   d. Net Present Value

**11.** A company that is highly geared has a high proportion of its finance in the form of:
   a. Investments
   b. Profits
   c. Loans
   d. Cash

**12.** Which of the following are internal sources of finance for a firm?
   I.   Retained Profits
   II.  Funding from family and friends
   III. Bank overdraft
   IV.  Sale of assets
   a. I, II
   b. I, III
   c. I, IV
   d. I, II, III, IV

**13.** Goodwill can be BEST described as:
   I.   Intangible assets
   II.  It arises from a firm's good reputation
   III. A firm's established brand name
   IV.  The good relations a firm has with workers
   a. I only
   b. II, IV
   c. I, III, IV
   d. I, II, III

**14.** A main drawback of leasing is that:
   a. The firm can buy the asset at the end of the contracted term
   b. The lessee can sell the asset
   c. The asset is not owned by the lessee
   d. The lessee can acquire the asset without the need for the initial cash outlays of purchasing the asset

# Unit 2
## Module 1

## Production and operations management

# Nature of production

## Objectives

At the end of this section you will know:

1. The major decisions involved in the production process
2. Different production methods
3. Factors affecting the location of a firm.

## Production

1. Production is the process whereby a firm uses various factors of production to convert raw materials into finished goods and services to meet consumer demand.
2. Input refers to the factors of production that a firm would use to make its good or service.
3. Factors of production include: land, labour, capital and enterprise. They are converted to form the final product. The production process is called the throughput and gives the final product which is the output, that is, the end product.

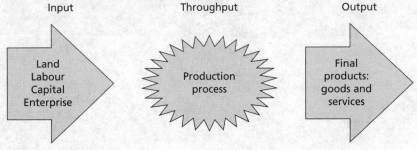

The production process

4. The aim of the production department is to provide high-quality goods in the required quantity at the lowest possible cost to meet consumer demand.
5. In order to achieve this objective the firm has to decide what to produce.
6. A market-oriented firm will use the results of its market research to determine consumers' demands.
7. In order to decide what to produce the firm will need to know:
   a. The market segment targeted
   b. The nature of the market, i.e. level of competition, etc.
   c. How to design the product
   d. The selling price
   e. How to promote the product
   f. How to distribute the product.
8. The production-oriented firm will use its market research to develop the product. It is believed that if the product is of high quality then consumers will demand the product.
9. Value analysis
   a. This is a technique for evaluating the effectiveness of producing a product. The objective is to produce a product at the lowest cost that will also meet consumer requirements.
   b. In designing a new product, managers must ensure the product satisfies consumers demand. This is achieved by all managers working together.

### The product design

When designing a new product the following must be considered:

1. Performance: the product must have the performance capabilities consumers would expect.
2. Appearance: the product must be attractive.
3. Cost of production: the cost of production must be cost-effective. This will guarantee sales and ensure a high profit margin.
4. Tools and techniques: the production manager can use a variety of techniques to ensure a high level of production in the firm; e.g. Just-in-Time method of stock control and the use of critical path analysis.
5. Stock control: managers must ensure that stocks are available when needed and finished products reach the consumer in a timely manner.
6. The external environment: production managers must also be aware of the trade cycle. For example, in an inflationary period, prices will be higher than in a recession. When consumers' disposable income falls, the cost of production must reflect these changes.

## Methods of production

There are different ways a product can be produced. These include the following:

1. **Job production**
2. **Batch production**
3. **Flow production**
4. **Cell production**

### 1. Job production

a. This involves producing a good or a service to cater for the specific needs of a consumer.
b. This type of production may be undertaken by small firms before they expand.
c. In this production process the firm does not benefit from economies of scale.
d. Job production increases consumer satisfaction as products meet their specific requirements.
e. Using job production for highly technical products can result in higher prices for consumers.
f. Normally, job production takes place on the premises where the product is made, e.g. building a house.
g. In some cases, the product must be completed on the site, e.g. shipbuilding.
h. Job production maintains a close relationship between the product and the consumer to ensure the consumer's specific needs are met. This will ensure consumer satisfaction and continued success for the product.
i. Profit margins tend to be high. The firm does not benefit from economies of scale. The time it takes to produce the product means there is a higher cost to the consumer and higher profits for the producer. In job production, each individual product is normally completed before the next product is started.

Hairdressing is a job production service that must meet the specific requirements of the consumer

| Advantages and disadvantages of job production | |
|---|---|
| **Advantages** | **Disadvantages** |
| › It motivates the producer as they see the product from its beginning to its completion | › Cost would be higher for the consumer |
| › Profit margin is higher for each unit produced | › Time taken to produce the output is longer |
| › It caters for the specific needs of the consumer | › It requires a highly skilled workforce and this is not always easy to obtain |
| › The close relationship that develops between consumers and producer may mean continued business for the producer | |

### 2. Batch production

Bread manufacturing is a batch production process

a. In batch production, the product goes through a series of distinct stages and each stage of production is highly planned. Each must be completed before the next stage can begin. Each product must go through each stage before the batch as a whole is completed.
b. One feature of batch production is that after a batch has been completed, the entire process must be started again; this may mean that time will be wasted.

c. In this type of production, groups of identical products move through the different stages of production at the same time.

d. It is used, for example, in the baking industry where a batch of chocolate chip cookies may be baked at one time; after which another batch of cookies such as peanut cookies will be made.

e. Batch production allows the firm to benefit from the same economies of scale as job production but fewer than flow production.

f. The firm can benefit from division of labour when using batch production. This is not possible in job production.

g. Each batch of output may cater for the specific needs of the consumer.

| Advantages and disadvantages of batch production | |
|---|---|
| Advantages | Disadvantages |
| › It allows the firm to use division of labour | › The production process can be boring for workers because it includes the division of labour. Workers may do the same task for the entire day. This could mean that workers lack interest in their jobs; there is a likelihood of increased errors and a fall in productivity |
| › The firm benefits from economies of scale. This means the cost of production will fall. Selling price will fall. Demand will increase. Profits will increase | › Workers become demotivated as they cannot identify with the finished product |
| › It allows the firm to cater for the specific needs of the consumer and various market segments; e.g., in the case of cookies, the segment that will demand coconut cookies or peanut cookies | › Cost of production may be higher because of limited benefits of economies of scale |
| | › The time taken to reset machines as the firm moves from producing one batch to another may mean there is a fall in productivity from both workers and machines. This will have a negative effect on the firm's profit margin |

## 3. Flow production

a. Flow production is a production process where products move from one stage of production to another stage continuously.

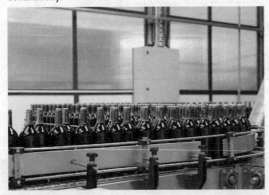

Beer bottling is a flow production process. It is capital intensive.

b. Flow production is capital intensive. It is suitable where there is a high demand for the firm's output.

c. Firms can reap the benefits of economies of scale. Cost of production will fall. Selling price will fall. Demand will increase and the firm will gain increased profits.

| Advantages and disadvantages of flow production ||
|---|---|
| **Advantages** | **Disadvantages** |
| › Flow production is capital intensive. Labour cost is therefore low. The product flows from one stage to another, with very little contact by workers | › There is little variation in the products, as they are produced on a large scale |
| › A large volume of identical products are produced. The firm receives all the benefits of economies of scale | › This production process, because it is capital intensive, can be boring for workers. This will mean managers may have to implement strategies to motivate workers |
| › Flow production allows for standardised products to be produced. The makes it easier for quality to be maintained as it can be monitored at each stage of the production process | › High costs are incurred in setting up the production process. In addition, there are high costs of servicing and replacing worn out equipment |
| › There is no need to keep a large stock of finished goods. | › If machines break down, the entire production process must be stopped until the necessary repairs have been made. The firm may not be able to keep the delivery date for its output. This could mean customers will seek other suppliers |
| › It saves time – there is no need to move from one point in the factory to another. | › The production process can be boring for workers and demotivating for them. This increases the level of accidents, absenteeism and labour turnover, all of which contributes to higher costs for the producer |

## 4. Cell production

  a. Cell production is a method of production in which the manufacturing process is organised into independent units or cells.

  b. Cell production is a form of flow production. The main difference is that cell production involves setting up separate self-contained small production units, called cells.

  c. In this production process, teams of workers, the machines they require and all inputs required for production are grouped together in the production site.

  d. Each cell has a structure. In charge of each cell is the leader; below the leader are the workers.

  e. All workers in the cell are multi-skilled. This ensures high levels of output, increased efficiency and productivity.

  f. Working as a team results in improved communication and workers become more motivated.

  g. Advantages of cell production

  Cell production allows workers to function as a team and therefore enjoy the benefits of:

  i. Increased levels of communication

  ii. Increased levels of motivation

  iii. Sharing of ideas to establish best practices

  iv. Implementing policies and, by extension, improving the efficiency and productivity of the firm.

## Location

1. **One of the most significant decisions managers have to make is where to locate a business. This has a direct impact on the profitability of the firm. Location decisions are strategic and are not easily reversed.**

2. **There are a number of factors a manager must consider when deciding where to locate. These include the following:**

  a. Quantitative factors

  b. Qualitative factors

3. **Quantitative factors**

  The following quantitative factors affect the firm's choice of location:

  a. Costs of location

  b. All businesses will examine the costs of a number of locations before making the final decision to locate. These costs are likely to include:

  i. Purchase or lease of the site

  ii. Cost of rent

  iii. Cost of labour

  iv. Cost of electricity

c. Transport costs: firms will want to locate where transport cost is lowest.
   i. If the raw material is heavy and bulky, in order to reduce transport cost, firms will locate close to the raw materials.
   ii. If the firm offers a service, e.g. hairdressing, it will locate close to its market, e.g. in the urban areas.

d. Cost of raw materials: this will be high if raw materials have to be transported over long distances. If inputs are heavy and bulky, the firm is likely to locate close to the raw material.

e. Closeness to market: Firms will locate close to their markets:
   i. This would reduce their cost of transportation
   ii. The selling price of goods and services will fall
   iii. Demand for their output will increase
   iv. Profit margins will increase

f. Available supply of cheap labour: firms will locate where there is a ready supply of cheap labour. This will reduce the cost of production. Relocating workers is expensive. Cost of training workers is expensive.

g. Where the revenue obtained is greater than the cost of production: firms will be established where the aggregate cost of production is less than the revenue obtained from its operation. This is so because in the long-run all firms will want to maximise profits.

h. Firms will also locate in areas where the government may offer incentives for location.

4. **Qualitative factors**

The following are the **qualitative factors** that affect the location of a firm.

a. Infrastructure: the presence of adequate infrastructure will be a pull factor for firms. They will locate where the transport system is adequate, where there are proper roads, bridges, an adequate supply of water, information technology and an adequate energy supply.

b. Environmental factors: these must be considered in order to prevent the actions of pressure groups. Firms have a social responsibility to preserve the environment. Firms that have high levels of negative externalities should be located away from residential areas. In the Caribbean, there are laws that seek to ensure the environment remains healthy both for the people and as a means of attracting investors.

c. Planning consideration: before deciding where to locate, management need to be aware of all the rules and regulations that must be observed. For example, what laws govern the proposed project? What will be the cost of doing business in the area? How long will it take to get approval for the business to actually start? Firms will tend to locate where there is ease in doing business.

d. Management preference: management will want to locate in areas where there is a better quality of life, i.e., in areas that offer better health services, sporting amenities, shopping facilities and opportunities for social and cultural development and a low crime rate.

e. Globalisation and location: globalisation has made it possible for firms to explore locations across international borders. Firms will want to locate where:
   i. Exchange rate is low
   ii. Rate of interest is competitive
   iii. There is political stability
   iv. There are no language barriers
   v. The government offers adequate incentives to attract investors
   vi. Firms can repatriate their profits
   vii. Crime rate is low.

 QUICK TEST

1. **State the quantitative factors affecting the location of a firm.**                 **[15 marks]**
2. **State the qualitative factors affecting the location of a firm.**                  **[15 marks]**
3. **Discuss with the aid of examples the advantages of:**
   a. Job production                                                                    **[15 marks]**
   b. Batch production                                                                  **[15 marks]**
   c. Flow production                                                                   **[15 marks]**
   d. Cell production                                                                   **[15 marks]**

# Forecasting techniques

## Objectives

At the end of this section you will know the various forecasting techniques a firm can employ.

It is important for firms to be able to forecast the demand for their output with some measure of accuracy. This is necessary to ensure survival, growth and expansion of the firm.

The following are the forecasting techniques a firm can use.

### a. Sales force composite
1. In the sales force composite method of forecasting demand, each member of the sales team will give a forecast of expected sales for their respective areas.
2. The submission from each sale representative is added to arrive at the firm's future potential demand for its product.
3. Sales representatives are in close contact with retail outlets and can therefore predict market trends.

### b. The Delphi method
1. The Delphi method is a qualitative forecasting technique.
2. It is based on the results of a questionnaire obtained from a panel of experts.
3. The experts do not meet. They are not directly employed by the business.
4. In the first instance the questionnaires are given out to experts.
5. The results are summarised and another questionnaire sent out to the panel to review their previous position.
6. There may be many rounds before a final decision is made. The procedure is stopped when a consensus is reached.
7. The advantage of this forecasting technique is that the views of the panel members are independent.
8. The disadvantage is that the process is costly and time consuming.

### c. Consumer surveys
1. The consumer survey is the most frequently used method of forecasting demand. It is a bottom-up approach. It involves the projected target market.
2. It can be quantitative or qualitative.
3. It can be conducted by face-to-face interviews or questionnaire given to consumers.
4. It is important that the sample of consumers used is large enough to be representative of the target market.
5. The advantage of a consumer survey is that it involves one actual consumer's point of view.
6. The disadvantage is the cost involved in preparing the questionnaire.

### d. Jury of experts
1. The jury of experts is made up of experts who are directly employed by the business.
2. This is a top-down method of forecasting demand. Senior managers attempt to forecast demand based on their knowledge.
3. Here the experts may revise their opinions according to the opinion of the other experts.
4. Finally, a consensus is reached.
5. The advantage of a jury of experts to forecast demand is that experts in the field are used.
6. The disadvantage of this method is that some experts may follow one view expressed by a member of the team who may influence their decision.

### e. Moving average
1. A moving average shows how the average sales move over time.
2. All data can be divided into distinct categories. These include:
   i. Cyclical variations
   ii. Trend
   iii. Seasonal variations
   iv. Random variations

   i. **Cyclical variations**
      This applies only to annual data. Cyclical variations occur because of
      a) New firms entering the market
      b) The stage in the product's life cycle
      c) The trade cycle, i.e. the level of economic activity
   ii. **Trend**
      This is one general movement of the data. The forecast could show demand rising and falling, but if the percentage increase in forecasted demand is greater than the forecasted fall in demand then the general consensus is for an increasing demand.

iii. **Seasonal variation**

This refers to changes in sales data within a particular year; e.g. more rain coats are sold in the rainy seasons.

iv. **Random variations**

This is the part of the series that is difficult to predict.

3 The advantage of a moving average is that it takes into account seasonal variations. It is fairly accurate for forecasting demand in the short term.

4 The disadvantages are:

1. It is complex

2. Forecasts are based on part data and this sometimes is not accurate.

QUICK TEST

1. **Explain one Delphi method of forecasting demand.**                    [10 marks]

2. **Explain why a firm may use moving averages to forecast demand for its output.**          [10 marks]

3. **Discuss why a firm would want to forecast the demand for its output.**          [10 marks]

# Product design strategies

## Objectives

At the end of this section you will know the various design strategies a firm can use to produce a product.

## Introduction

There are a number of strategies a firm can use in the design of its product, all of which have the single objective of increasing the demand for the product.

Consumers get value for their money, which increases the firm's profit margin. Production design strategies involve each department in the firm. Production design strategies are as follows.

1. **Modularisation**
   a. A given product or unit is manufactured so that other parts can be easily added to this main unit or taken away. The objective is to create a product that can cater for the specific needs of a market segment.
   b. For example, a manufacturer of kitchen supplies will manufacture a basic unit. To this unit the manufacturer may offer additions for slicing, kneading, juicing to cater for different market segments.
   c. The unit may be sold with or without the additions to meet the demand of different market segments.
   d. For modularisation to be successful the electrical and mechanical links between the modules must facilitate these additions.
   e. Advantages of modularisation:
      i. It becomes easier to improve the product. The basic product remains the same and changes are made to given modules. This is easier to do. The improved product can them be sold to the market as a new improved product.
      ii. Each component can be manufactured and tested separately before the final product is assembled. Errors can therefore be detected and rectified.
      iii. A wider range of products can be sold to consumers. Modularisation allows for additions to the main unit. This would be impossible if the product were standardised.
      iv. The firm is able to cater to various segments of the market; e.g consumers who want a standard product as well as those who demand a non-standard product.

2. **Miniaturisation**
   a. Miniaturisation is the process whereby firms make their products smaller and, at the same time, include additional features; for example, the computer today is in fact a miniature of the original computer, yet is more powerful.
   b. In order to achieve miniaturisation very high levels of technology are employed.
   c. The firms therefore are capital intensive. This means they receive the benefits of economies of scale.
   d. Costs of production therefore fall and by extension the selling price also falls as demand increases.
   e. Advantages of miniaturisation:
      i. Production costs falls. The firms are capital intensive. Selling price falls. Consumer pays less for the product.
      ii. The product now has more features, e.g. the cell phone
      iii. The product becomes more convenient to handle
      iv. They are easier to dispose of. They are more environmentally friendly

3. **Integration**
   In order for a product to be successful, all departments in the firm must have an input in its production to achieve the firm's objective. Success therefore is in fact an integration of the other departments in the firm.
   a. The marketing department plays a vital role in conducting the necessary market research to determine the market share and unique selling points of competitors. They conduct sales research into the position of the product.
   b. The finance department must have the necessary finance for the market research; to purchase new equipment and pay additional staff if these are necessary.
   c. The human resources department will have to provide the necessary staff. This may mean employing additional staff or providing the necessary training for existing staff if this is needed.
   d. The production department, in conjunction with the other departments, will then design and manufacture a product that meets the need of consumers and the objectives of the firm.
   e. This will translate into a marketable product and huge profit margin for the firm.

4. **Value analysis**
   a. Value analysis is a technique used by firms for evaluating the effectiveness of producing its products.
   b. The main objective of value analysis is to produce a product that caters for consumers' needs, but at a lower cost.

   c. To achieve a lower cost of production the firm may need to:

     i. Redesign its product

     ii. Look for cheaper sources of raw material

     iii. Alter the manufacturing process

   d. However, these must not be achieved at the expense of performance and aesthetics.

   e. The firm will therefore have to create value in relation to the cost of production.

## 5. Computer aided design (CAD)

   a. CAD involves the use of computers to aid in designing a product.

   b. The designer can then view a solid three-dimensional product instead of a series of drawings.

   c. Benefits of CAD:

     i. It saves times

     ii. It reduces the cost of the design process

     iii. It allows drawings to be stored and updated when needed

     iv. Designs can be tested

     v. Faults can be eliminated before the product is manufactured

   d. Firms in the packaging, motor vehicle as well as the aircraft industry benefit from CAD.

## 6. Computer aided manufacturing (CAM)

   a. CAM involves the use of computers as an integral part of the production process. It allows the use of computers to control machines.

   b. Computers are used to control the delivery of materials and components.

   c. Computers are used to control the operations of robots carrying out production activities.

   d. Benefits of CAM:

     i. It reduces costs to the firm.

     ii. It increases the level of productivity.

     iii. Quality is improved.

 QUICK TEST

**Define the following design strategies:**

| | |
|---|---|
| 1. Modularisation | [10 marks] |
| 2. Miniaturisation | [10 marks] |
| 3. Integration | [10 marks] |
| 4. Value analysis | [10 marks] |

# Capacity planning

## Objectives

At the end of this section you will know the:

1. **Importance of capacity utilisation**
2. **Methods of improving capacity utilisation**
3. **Advantages a firm gains as it increases in size**
4. **Limitations that an increase in size can have on the firm**

## Introduction

1. In order to produce at its lowest cost, firms must plan how to maximise the capacity available.
2. Capacity can be defined as the total level of output that a firm can produce in a given period of time using the same resources.
3. Immediate capacity measures the amount of output that can be produced with the current budget.
4. Effective capacity relates to the skills and abilities of the workers involved.

## Capacity utilisation

1. Capacity utilisation measures the extent to which the maximum capacity of the firm is being used; i.e. it measures actual output as a percentage of maximum potential output. Changes in demand and competitors' actions will affect the extent of capacity utilisation.

   Formula:

   $$\frac{\text{Actual output per period}}{\text{Full capacity per period}} \times 100$$

2. Using capacity as fully as possible would increase the firm's profitability. This is because the cost of production would be spread over a larger number of units. It can be measured on a daily, weekly or monthly basis.
3. Most firms attempt to achieve 90 per cent capacity utilisation.
4. At 100 per cent utilisation, no allowances would have been made to deal with emergencies.
5. Spare capacity is any capacity below the possible maximum level.

### Importance of capacity utilisation

1. A firm operating at 100 per cent capacity is using all of its inputs to the maximum.
   This may be desirable on the short-run but could be problematic in the long-run, unless allowances are made for work fatigue and maintenance of capital equipment within the calculation of 'potential output'.
2. Firms operating at zero capacity will still have to cover their fixed cost and will be making losses. Firms, therefore, will attempt to operate as close to their capacity as possible.
3. Firms can operate above full capacity in the short-run by:
   a) Rescheduling maintenance
   b) Working overtime
   c) Leasing additional machines
4. Capacity utilisation is important because:
   a. It allows the firm to gain the benefits of economies of scale
   b. It allows the unit cost of production to fall
   c. It enables the selling price to fall
   d. In a competitive market, demand for the firm's output will increase.
   e. It increases the firm's profit margin
   f. There is more capital for research and development, and to pay better wages, which leads to growth and expansion.
5. Working at near full capacity can also create pressures for the firm in terms of:
   a. Over-worked machinery
   b. Over-worked and tired labour force.
      This results in the firm not being able to take on additional work.
6. To cope with this, firms will have to employ part-time employees, lease extra machinery, and explore avenues to become more productive and efficient.

## Challenges associated with increased or full capacity utilisation

1. Reduced profits
2. Cost per unit of output increase
3. Firms may lose market share, as consumers turn to other suppliers
4. Difficult to re-establish links with suppliers when demand for their output increases
5. Workers become bored and frustrated
6. Workers may leave the firm

**Design capacity:** this measures the maximum output of a firm in a given time period of a day, a week, month.

## Capacity utilisation calculation:

The formula for calculating capacity utilisation is:

$$\text{Capacity utilisation} = \frac{\text{Output}}{\text{Potential output}} \times 100$$

**Effective capacity:** this refers to the maximum amount of output that a firm can actually achieve in a given time period. Effective capacity is therefore lower than design capacity.

## Methods of improving capacity utilisation

1. If a firm is producing below its full capacity, it is therefore not cost-effective. There are a number of strategies the firm can employ to improve its capacity utilisation.
2. When the supply of output is less than the quantity demanded by the market the following strategies can be employed:
   a. Employ an additional shift
   b. Make better use of resources
   c. Train workers where necessary
   d. Employ more efficient quality control measures
   e. Improve the production process, eliminating any possible downtime for machinery
3. If the firm is closer to full capacity and demand for the firm's output is greater than supply the options are:
   a. Expand the firm
   b. Purchase additional machinery
   c. Employ additional highly qualified staff
   d. Train and retrain existing staff
4. If there is excess capacity because potential supply is greater than demand:
   a. The marketing department would develop strategies to increase demand
   b. Lease part of the production area
   c. Lay off workers or reduce the hours they work
   d. Sell equipment that is not being used.

# Economies of scale

Economies of scale are the benefits a firm gains as it increases in size. Economies of scale can be internal or external.

## Internal economies of scale

Internal economies of scale are the benefits the firm gains as it grows in size. The following gains are made as the firm increases its output.

1. **Division of labour and specialisation:** the larger the firm the greater is the opportunity for specialisation. In larger firms the entire operation can be broken down, e.g. functional departments can be set up employing specialists.
2. **Technical economies:** the firm can now purchase specialist equipment and machinery
3. **Purchasing economies:** firms can purchase in bulk at a lower cost
4. **Financial economies:** firms can obtain loans easier and at a lower rate of interest
5. **Bulk bearing economies:** large firms may be able to diversify their output. If the demand for one product fails, the firm can cross subsidise using the profits from another product to offset the loss of the failing product.
6. **Marketing economies:** the cost of marketing a large volume of output will be reduced as cost will be spread over a larger quantity of output

## External economies of scale

External economies of scale are the benefits a firm gains as the industry grows. These include:

1. **Information:** large industries would have information that is designed to assist workers. The firms can pool resources to conduct research and development that will benefit the entire industry.
2. **Disintegration:** as a firm grows in size, other firms may locate close to it to provide the necessary inputs at a low cost; e.g. maintenance firms to repair equipment or others providing catering services.
3. **Better local infrastructure:** water supply, better roads, power supply.
4. **The supply of labour is improved.**
5. **Suppliers may begin to locate near firms.** This allows for prompt delivery at a low cost.

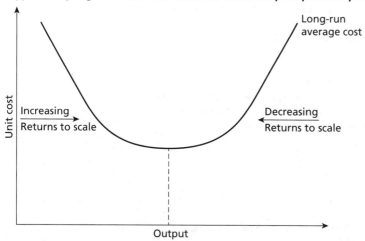

Returns to scale

## Diseconomies of scale

Diseconomies of scale are the disadvantages a firm experiences as it increases in size, e.g. the unit cost of production increases.

### Internal diseconomies of scale

As a firm grows, there can become a point where the cost of production increases.

1. **Management:** the size of firm may become too large for the existing managers to manage efficiently. This can lead to a rise in labour disputes and inefficiencies. The result is a higher cost of production.
2. **Decision-making may take longer.**
3. **The external environment:** if there is change in the external environment and demand for the firm's output falls, the firm will have spare capacity. This is a cost to the firm as prices will rise, leading to a fall in demand and consequently a fall in profits.

### External diseconomies of scale

1. **Competition for skilled labour:** firms operating in an industrial area, for example, may have to compete with each other for the limited supply of skilled labour. This would increase their cost of production.
2. **Increased cost:** as there is an increased demand for the factors of production, the prices of the factors will increase.
3. **Competition for market share:** as firms compete for market share, the cost of advertising will increase.

 QUICK TEST

1. Define economies of scale.                                                      [8 marks]
2. State and explain the internal economies of scale a firm can enjoy.             [15 marks]
3. State and discuss the internal diseconomies of scale a firm can experience.     [15 marks]

# Layout strategies

## Objectives

At the end of the review of this section you will know the:

1. **Different layouts a business can use**
2. **Advantages and disadvantages of each layout strategy.**

1. The layout of a factory must be structured to ensure the entire production process can take place in an environment that is conducive for workers. This would ensure the profitability of the firm.
2. The layout strategies are based on the objectives of the firm and the nature of the products being produced. To achieve this objective the layout should ensure that:
   a. In the production process there is as little movement of workers as possible
   b. The highest level of safety is achieved
   c. Security is at its highest at all times
   d. Coordination of the different departments can be achieved in a speedy manner
   e. Accessibility to machines and inputs would reduce production time and ensure a high level of productivity
   f. There is a high level of visibility. This would prevent accidents and reduce cost to the firm
3. There are a number of layout strategies a firm can use. These include:
   a. Process layout
   b. Production layout
   c. Fixed position layout
   d. Cellular layout

## Process layout

1. **Process layout is characterised by clustering all machines performing similar tasks.**
2. **Using this type of layout enables different types of products to pass through the system.**
3. **It ensures a more efficient use of machinery.**
4. **If there is a breakdown of one machine, there are others to be used so production is not affected.**

| Advantages and disadvantages of process layout | |
|---|---|
| **Advantages** | **Disadvantages** |
| › Workers become highly specialised in the function or process they are involved in | › There is not a continuous flow of work for the various processes and as a result workers may be forced to remain idle as they wait for the various departments to send work to be done |
| › Workers' productivity will increase | › Process layout can lead to the firm having a pile up of work-in-progress. This is because all output must pass through the various processes or departments before completion |
| › Flexible process layout will allow for many different product routes | › If the firm is providing a service it is important that the aisles are large to accommodate the free movement of customers as accidents can occur |
| › It ensures a high utilisation of machinery and there is a back-up of machinery to cater for any possible breakdown of machinery | |

## Production layout

1. **The firm structures its layout according to the requirements of the production process in a given sequence.**
2. **Movement from one stage of production to another stage is in a sequence. There is therefore an easy flow.**
3. **Each product has its own production line based on its given sequence.**
4. **This type of layout is suitable for firms where the demand for its output is high.**
5. **Flow production technique uses this method layout.**

| Advantages and disadvantages of production layout | |
|---|---|
| **Advantages** | **Disadvantages** |
| › Unit cost of production is low, as the firm benefits from economies of scale | › If there is a problem in one area of production it may mean that this will delay the entire process |
| › There is a high level of efficiency. This would reduce the cost of production and reduce the selling price. The demand for the firm's output will therefore increase | › It can only be employed where the demand for the firm's output is high |
| › It allows workers to become specialists in their given area | |
| › Handling time is reduced | |
| › Work is broken down and made simpler | |
| › Control of the production process is therefore more effective | |

## Fixed position layout

1. In fixed position layout the machinery and equipment are in a fixed position to enable production to take place.
2. When production is completed the products are taken to a storage area or delivered to wholesalers or retailers.
3. Fixed position layout is also used in the construction industry. The construction of houses and ships must take place in a fixed location; materials, machines and workers are brought to this fixed location.
4. This layout strategy is used where the item being produced is too heavy to move.
5. Equipment, workers and materials are all brought to a given location.
6. Fixed position layout will require workers who are skilled in various activities. Some workers will be employed for the entire duration of the project. Other workers may be employed for shorter periods.
7. Fixed position layout is also used where the product is fragile so that it must be produced on site.
8. A disadvantage is that time could be wasted if materials do not arrive when needed. This would mean increased costs of production.

## Cellular layout

1. Cellular layout involves dividing the factory into small units, called cells.
2. Each cell consists of multi-skilled workers and a team leader who work as a team to produce a finished product, or part of a product.
3. Each cell is involved in the production of a group of products which require the same sequence of operations.
4. Production is tailored to suit the skill of the worker.
5. Workers in each cell are motivated as they are multi-skilled, so production does not become boring and because they can identify with the finished product.
6. There is a high level of productivity in cellular production. Suppliers and customers may be external to the firm, or internal where the output of one cell becomes the input of another cell.
7. Advantages of cellular layout:
   a. Cell production layout requires less space than other production layouts. This mean there is greater freedom of movement for staff.
   b. Productivity would increase as workers are all multi-skilled.
   c. There is better communication among workers, which leads to increased levels of motivation.
   d. Preparation time is reduced.
   e. There is improved efficiency as a result of standardization and simplification of output.
   f. There is a reduction in stocks.
   g. There is less work-in-progress, as each cell may be responsible for a complete product.

 QUICK TEST

1. What are the advantages of cellular manufacturing to a firm?                    [10 marks]
2. Using an example, describe production layout as compared to fixed production layout.    [10 marks]
3. Using an example, explain what process layout is and state two of its advantages.    [10 marks]

# Costing

## Objectives

At the end of this section you will know the:

1. **Uses of break-even charts**
2. **Advantages of break-even analysis**
3. **Disadvantages of break-even analysis**
4. **Various approaches to costing.**

## Costs

1. **Direct cost or prime cost**
   a. Direct cost or prime cost are costs that can be directly allocated to the production of a particular good or product; for example, the cost of raw material
   b. For many manufactured products the firm can calculate direct labour cost, and raw material costs.

2. **Indirect costs or overheads**
   Indirect costs or overheads are costs that cannot be attributed to a particular product or processes.

3. **Variable costs (VC)**
   a. Variable costs are costs that change as the level of output changes; e.g. raw materials.
   b. As output increases total variable costs increase.
   c. Total variable costs (TVC) is variable cost per unit multiplied by the number of output produced:
   
   TVC = VC per unit × the number of units produced

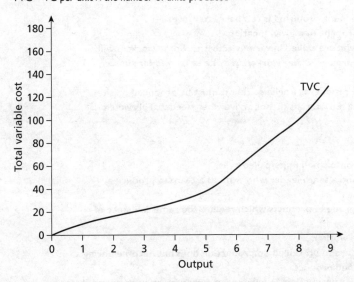

The Figure shows Total Variable Cost (TVC). TVC rises as output increases.

4. **Fixed cost (FC)**
   a. Fixed costs are costs that do not change when the firm alters its level of production, e.g. rent.
   b. Fixed cost must be paid whether the business is in operation or not.
   c. Fixed cost is a short-run concept.
   d. In the long term all cost are variable.

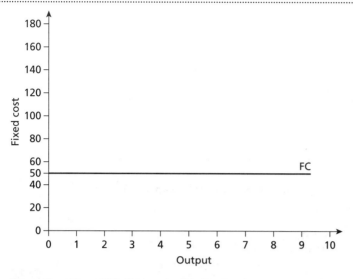

Figure: Fixed Cost, (FC). FC remains fixed in the short run.

5. **Total cost (TC)**

   Total cost is found by adding the fixed cost and the variable cost of production so:

   TC = FC + TVC

6. **As output rises so will total cost.**

7. **Average total cost (ATC)**

8. **This will fall as output rises because fixed costs are spread across more units of output.**

   $$ATC = \frac{TC}{Output}$$

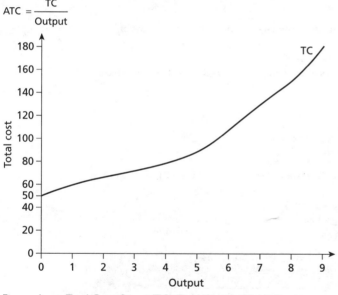

Figure shows Total Cost Curve (TC). Total Cost = FC + VC.

## Absorption costing (full cost or cost plus)

1. **Absorption costing includes all costs associated with the production of a particular product. It adds the direct labour cost and direct material costs.**

2. **It might be more difficult to determine how much of the indirect cost is identified with the particular production process.**

3. **Overhead cost therefore is divided by the expected units of output to find the overhead (indirect) cost per unit.**

   Full Cost = FC + VC + Profit Mark-Up

4. **Problems associated with absorption costing**

   a. It is not easy to forecast fixed costs in a multi-product firm.

   b. It assumes all output is sold.

   c. It ignores market conditions.

5. **Benefits associated with absorption costing**
   a. All costs are included.
   b. Absorption costing is arbitrary. The absorption rate is only valid if actual output was in keeping with budgeted output.
   c. It calculates the unit cost of an item after allocating a proportion of the estimated fixed overheads.
   d. Each unit must absorb its fair share of the overheads.
   e. It ensures price is set after all costs have been added.
   f. It requires an effective method for allocating overheads.

## Marginal costing/contribution

1. **Marginal costing can be defined as the addition to total cost resulting from production of an additional unit of output.**
2. **In calculating marginal cost the variable cost of producing an additional unit of output is involved in the calculations.**
3. **It ignores fixed costs.**
4. **It identifies the contribution from a particular activity.**
5. **Contribution is calculated by taking sales minus variable cost; i.e.**

   Contribution = Sales price – Variable cost per unit

6. **Contribution costing is used in transport. Cost is based only on the variable cost: i.e., it excludes any fixed costs.**
7. **It may involve some sales at less than full cost as long as other sales make more than full cost.**
8. **It is more likely to be used when:**
   a. The product is perishable.
   b. A sale below full cost will lead to increased market share.
   c. There is no alternative use for equipment or labour which would otherwise be underemployed.
   d. Fixed costs are a large proportion of total cost.

## Break even

1. **Break even is the level of output at which the revenue earned by a firm is equal to the cost of producing that product.**
2. **At this point the firm is neither making a profit nor a loss.**
3. **The break-even chart shows the costs and revenues of the firm and allows the level of break-even output to be identified.**
4. **Break even can be calculated by the formula:**

$$\text{Break-even output} = \frac{\text{Fixed cost}}{\text{Selling price per unit} - \text{Variable cost per unit}}$$

5. **The concept of contribution is used in determining break even.**
6. **Break even calculates the level of output where total revenue = total costs (TR = TC); i.e. the firm is making neither a profit nor a loss.**
7. **If operating above break even, the firm is making a profit.**
8. **If operating below break even, the firm is making a loss.**
9. **Advantages vs disadvantages of break-even analysis**

| Advantages and disadvantages of break-even analysis | |
|---|---|
| **Advantages** | **Disadvantages** |
| › It is valuable for small and newly established firms | › Some costs are difficult to classify as fixed costs or variable costs |
| › Managers in multi-product firms are assisted in making decisions by giving an overview of the entire business | › Pricing decisions based on contribution do not take the conditions present in the market |
| › It eliminates the arbitrary division of fixed cost | › In the long-term fixed costs can change; this will make any earlier decisions based on contribution invalid |
| › Contribution can provide a flexible basis for the firm's pricing decisions | › The information used to construct the graph may not be reliable |

| | |
|---|---|
| › It is used by firms to aid in decision-making, e.g:<br>  o whether to produce a new product<br>  o whether to start trading<br>  o the likely profits or losses resulting from sales<br>    forecast | › Sales and output may not be exactly the same |
| › It aids managers as they analyse the effect of changes in the cost of inputs on the profitability of the firm | › The analysis is static. Whenever there is a change in any variables a new graph must be drawn |
| › It is a valuable tool in deciding whether the firm should accept an order for products at prices different from those normally charged | |
| › It can show the different level of profit among firms from different levels of output and sales | |
| › It is quick and easy to complete | |

10. **Assumptions in calculating break even**
    a. Costs are either fixed or variable
    b. All units of output are sold at the same price
    c. All output produced in a period is sold at that period
    d. There is no change in the variable cost of each unit of output
    e. Fixed costs remain fixed across a range of output
11. **Break-even level of output can be reduced by:**
    a. Reducing the fixed cost
    b. Reducing the variable cost per unit
    c. Increasing prices

## Contribution per unit

1. **Contribution per unit shows how much the sale of one product will contribute to the fixed costs of a firm.**
2. **When the fixed costs have been covered, sales of the product contribute to profit.**
   It is calculated as follows:
   Contribution per unit = Selling price – Direct cost per unit
3. **The total contribution of a product can be calculated in the following ways:**
   › Contribution per unit × Number of units sold
   › Total sales revenue – Total direct costs

## Margin of safety

1. **Margin of safety is the amount by which a business's current level of production exceeds the level required to break even.**
2. **It allows firms to judge by how much their production and sales can decline before they begin to experience a loss.**
   Formula:

$$\text{Margin of safety} = \frac{\text{Actual sales} - \text{break-even sales}}{\text{Actual sales}} \times 100$$

**Break-even charts:**

## Make or buy decisions

1. A very important decision a firm must make is whether to make a product or buy it. In coming to a decision a number of factors must be taken into account. Whether the firm makes the product or buys it depends on the firm's cost-benefit analysis. Benefits must be greater than cost.

2. The following are some reasons why a firm will want to make its own products:

   a. To maintain its quality. The reputation of the firm is at stake.

   b. Costs will be lower. Outsourcing will be more costly.

   c. The firm has spare capacity. If plant and equipment are being underutilised then the firm can benefit from full capacity utilisation.

   d. There are no suitable suppliers. In this situation the firm must produce the product itself.

   e. The size of the order. It may not be cost-effective for another firm to accept this order.

   f. Delivery times. The outside supplier may not be able to deliver the supplies on time.

   g. To maintain secrecy. In a highly competitive market it is vital that the firm keeps its operations secret.

   h. To ensure a ready supply of output. This is necessary to ensure customer loyalty and maintain market share.

   i. To give workers employment. This is vital if workers have been with the firm for long periods and it will be a cost factor to lay off workers and then have to retrain new staff when needed.

3. The following are the factors that will lead a firm to outsource supplies:

   a. The lack of spare capacity: if the firm is operating at full capacity.

   b. The cost factor: it is more cost-effective to buy the product than make it.

   c. The lack of technical skill to make the product: it would not be cost-effective to hire the technical skills.

   d. To increase specialisation: if the product needed is not in keeping with the firm's line of operation, it is prudent to outsource the product. This allows the firm to specialise in its line of output.

   e. The credibility of the outside firm: if the firm can depend on the efficiency as well as the quality of the output of the outside firm.

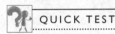 QUICK TEST

1. Draw and label a break-even chart.                                                    [10 marks]
2. Discuss the advantages of using break-even analysis.                                  [10 marks]
3. Discuss the disadvantages of using break-even analysis.                               [10 marks]

# Inventory management

## Objectives

At the end of this section you will:

1. **Know the reasons for holding stocks**
2. **Know the role of stock control**
3. **Be able to compare Just-in-time with the re-order system of stock control**

## Inventory management

1. **Most firms will attempt to minimise the amount of stocks they hold as a means of reducing costs. For some firms, holding stocks is necessary. The stock held consists of:**
   a. Raw materials and components
   b. Work-in-progress. These are partly finished goods
   c. Finished goods. This consists of the firm's output held to cope with fluctuations in demand. Stocks will be built-up in periods of low demand and run down during periods of high demand.
2. **Cost of holding stock**
   a. Money is tied up in stock. This could affect the cash flow of the business.
   b. Large areas of the plant would be used to hold stock
   c. Stock could become obsolete
   d. High cost of holding stock: pilfering, heating light and insurance cost are included.

## Stock control

1. **What is stock control?**
   Stock control refers to the techniques and procedures that are necessary to ensure that stocks are ordered and delivered in a timely fashion.
2. **The role of stock control**
   There are a number of reasons why it is important for a firm to control its stock levels. These include the following:
   a. To control the amount of money tied up in stock
   b. To ensure the firm has an adequate level of stock for production
   c. To control wastage
   d. To control pilferage
   e. For valuation purposes.
3. **Reasons for holding stock**
   There are a number of reasons why firms hold stock. These include the following:
   a. They have the necessary storage space
   b. There is not the likelihood that stocks will become outdated
   c. The firm will receive the economies of bulk buying
   d. To run the plant more efficiently by keeping production at a steady rate
   e. As a precaution against disruption, e.g. strikes, transport problems affecting suppliers
   f. If the firm anticipates an increase in price of the stock
   g. If the firm anticipates an increase in demand for its output, i.e. prevent stock-outs
   h. The financial position of the firm. The money for purchasing the stock is available.
4. **The implications of stock holding**
   a. The amount of stock held will reflect the nature of the good: low levels of stock if the good is perishable
   b. The market being served: if it is seasonal
   c. Production process: a chemical plant will need adequate supplies of raw material to maintain continuous production.
5. **Benefits of holding stock**
   a. The firm can produce even if the supplier fails to deliver.
   b. The firm can produce even if machines break down.
   c. The firm can sell even if its production process has stopped.

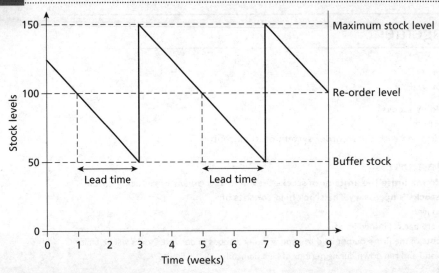

**A model for stock holding**

6. **The re-order level:** this level of stock will indicate to management to place an order for more stock.
7. **The economic order quantity:** this is the difference between the minimum and maximum stock levels
8. **The minimum stock level or buffer stock:** this is the minimum of stock the firm should have to ensure a supply of stock is always available
9. **The maximum stock level:** this includes the economic order quantity (EOQ) plus the minimum level. Any amount of stock held above the level would increase the cost of holding stock.
10. **Lead time:** this is the difference between placing an order and the delivery of the order.
11. **The economic order quantity (EOQ)**

It is defined as the ordering of quantity which minimises the balance of cost of holding stocks and the re-order costs.
The EOQ can be calculated using the formula:

$$\sqrt{\frac{2pd}{c}}$$

Where, $p$ = procurement cost
      $d$ = annual use of the material
      $c$ = cost of holding stock per year

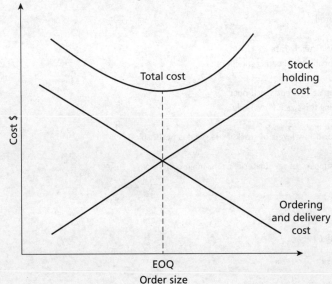

## Just-In-Time

1. Just-in-Time (JIT) is a stock control system associated with Japanese management.
2. Materials arrive exactly when needed.
3. Raw materials and inventories are reduced to zero.

4. Work-in-progress is kept to a minimum.
5. Investment in working capital is reduced.
6. Shop floor is less clustered with work-in-progress.
7. To be successful, there must be a well-coordinated production system.
8. JIT is a demand-pull system; each work station produces output only when it is needed by the next station.
9. JIT requires precise scheduling with coordination to avoid stock-outs to ensure that inputs arrive wherever needed in a fast and efficient manner.
10. It is imperative that workers are efficient and well-motivated.
11. JIT requires exact scheduling with total coordination to avoid bottlenecks.
12. JIT requires effective communication.
13. JIT requires the labour force to be capable of checking for and correcting problems when they occur.
14. JIT requires a flexible workforce.
15. JIT requires good labour relations.
16. JIT requires regular demand for its output.
17. JIT requires a large capital outlay on a computerised stock control system using Kanban.

| Advantages and disadvantages of Just-In-Time | |
|---|---|
| **Advantages** | **Disadvantages** |
| › It reduces waste in the firm. Stock does not become obsolete. This is because materials are ordered only when there is the demand for them. Stocks are not allowed to pile up. A reduction in waste means the firm becomes more efficient. This translates into higher profits for the firms | › Just-in-time depends heavily on the fact that suppliers will deliver inputs when needed. This can be to the disadvantage of the firm if for some reason the selected suppliers cannot make that prompt delivery |
| › There is more factory space. This could reduce the incidence of accidents; these are a cost to the firm in terms of worker absenteeism and a consequent fall in productivity | › It will be difficult for the firm to cater for an increase in demand. This is because the firm does not hold stocks of raw materials, semi-finished products or finished products. This is a disadvantage as the firm will lose potential profits and more importantly a potentially new customer |
| › The cost of holding stocks is reduced. This cost includes: high insurance cost, costs of pilfering, stocks becoming obsolete, warehousing, lighting and heating, air conditioning | › Just-in-time involves buying inputs only when needed. It means there may not be bulk buying if orders are relatively small. The firm therefore may not be able to benefit from economies of scale. Cost of production will be higher |
| › It requires a close relationship with suppliers, who are asked to supply, e.g., inputs of high quality wherever needed. There is a more integrated approach to the entire production process. All departments must be working closely to achieve the necessary success | › Since there is no stock of raw materials, semi-finished products or finished products, if for some reason the suppliers are delayed, this creates a problem in the firm's production process and delivery cannot be prompt, and there is the possibility that customers will seek other suppliers |
| › Workers are more motivated. JIT requires that workers work in teams, communication is improved, and there is less chance of conflict as workers are given more responsibility. This too will improve morale in the firm | › Transport cost is high, as orders are made more frequently. In addition, for each order there is the additional administration cost |
| › The firm is less likely to experience a cash flow problem. Money is not tied up in stock. When stocks are requested they are purchased in relation to the existing demand | |
| › The number of suppliers is reduced to include only those who are reliable and efficient. That is, those who can supply when needed | |

 QUICK TEST

**Explain the following terms:**

1. Economic order quantity　　　　　　　　　　　　　　　　[10 marks]
2. Buffer stock　　　　　　　　　　　　　　　　　　　　　　[10 marks]
3. Re-order level　　　　　　　　　　　　　　　　　　　　　[10 marks]
4. Minimum stock level　　　　　　　　　　　　　　　　　　[10 marks]
5. Maximum stock level　　　　　　　　　　　　　　　　　　[10 marks]

# Lean production and quality management

## Objectives
At the end of this section you will:
1. **Know the dimensions of quality**
2. **Know the ways a firm can improve the quality of its output**
3. **Understand the concept of lean production as it relates to inventory management, quality and capacity and employees rates.**

It is important that the output of a firm meets the needs of consumers. Quality is determined by the consumer. It is based on their needs and expectations of the good or service produced. The quality of a product will determine if consumers will buy the product and keep on buying it.

### The importance of quality to a firm
1. **Top quality products give the firm a competitive advantage in the market.**
2. **It will increase sales.**
3. **It can increase market share.**
4. **It reduces costs to the firm in terms of providing a replacement or the cost to repair a defective product.**
5. **It endorses the reputation of the firm.**
6. **It makes it easier for the firm to introduce new products to the market.**

### Dimensions of quality
The following are the dimensions of quality that determines if consumers will demand the product.
1. **Performance: Does the product perform its function? This dimension of quality can be measured in terms of its performance.**
2. **Features: these are added to the basic product. These features must be identifiable and measurable, e.g. a cell phone with a camera as the added feature.**
3. **Reliability: this applies to durable consumer goods. The reliability of a product is determined by how long it takes before the product fails.**
4. **Conformance: this is the extent to which a product meets the required specifications.**
5. **Durability: This is a measure of the life of the product, i.e. the number of uses the consumer gets from the product before it malfunctions.**
6. **Serviceability: How easy it is to have the item repaired. Are the service personnel polite? Are the service personnel able to repair the product?**
7. **Aesthetics: this is subjective. Not every consumer will agree, for example, on the look of a product.**
8. **Perceived quality: this is based on, for example, brand image or advertising.**

## Difference between quality control and quality assurance
There is a difference between quality control and quality assurance.

### Quality assurance
1. **Quality assurance is a technique used by firms to ensure that all products leaving the firm are of top quality and have met established quality standards. It includes quality control and consists of various activities in a business, all aimed at quality.**
2. **The technique is based on preventing poor quality products from leaving the firm.**
3. **It is the responsibility of each worker to ensure that quality standards are achieved in the goods and services produced at each stage of production.**
4. **Quality assurance will involve the:**
   a. Quality of suppliers
   b. Commitment of the workers
   c. Delivery time for output
   d. Quality of advice and after-sales service
5. **Quality assurance involves the following areas:**
   a. Designing of the product: to meet consumers' taste.
   b. Quality of inputs: to guaranteed top quality.
   c. Quality of production: to ensure each work, plant and process meets quality standards.
   d. Delivery systems: to supply quality products in a timely manner.
   e. Consumer service: customer will give feedback on the quality of products.

6. **The benefits of quality assurance:**
   a. Each individual in the firm is responsible for maintaining quality. The workers are empowered.
   b. Workers are motivated so quality is improved.
   c. There are fewer errors or need to rework items produced.
   d. The main objective of quality assurance is to 'get it right the first time'.
   e. The cost of production falls

## Quality control

1. **Quality control differs from quality assurance in that quality assurance is based on prevention of poor quality goods and services.**
2. **Quality control is based on the corrective action a firm can take to achieve a quality established by the firm.**
3. **Quality control procedures take place after production is completed. This can be costly if the production process did, in fact, produce poor quality products.**
4. **Quality control inspectors are normally employed to verify quality.**
5. **Costs associated with quality control:**
   a. Materials scrapped
   b. Labour time wasted
   c. Rectifying poor work
   d. Inspection and measurement
   e. Training employees
   f. Loss of customer goodwill when poor quality output reaches the customers.
6. **It may therefore be cost-effective to employ quality assurance techniques to ensure consumers obtain not only top quality products but also at competitive prices.**
7. **Quality must be maintained at all stages of production:**
   a. Raw material must be of top quality.
   b. The plant and machinery must be functioning efficiently.
   c. Workers must be trained to use the technology.
   d. The product must be examined at each stage of the production process.
   e. Finished products must be examined before leaving the firm.
8. **The benefits of quality control:**
   a. At each stage in the production process, the product is inspected to ensure quality is maintained so it is unlikely that a defective product will reach the consumer.
   b. It is more secure than a system that relies on one individual to ensure quality.

## Techniques for improving quality

1. **Benchmarking**
   a. Benchmarking means setting performance standards of the firm in line with the best firms in the industry.
   b. It requires that the firm identifies the products or processes of the firm that are used as the benchmark before implementing the change in their own firm.
   c. Benchmarking involves:
      i. Identifying an area that is to be benchmarked
      ii. Measuring the performance of the firm before benchmarking
      iii. Setting a target for improvement
      iv. Making the necessary changes to achieve the targeted objective
      v. Measuring performance after benchmarking
2. **ISO Quality Standards**
   a. ISO is the International Organisation for Standardisation.
   b. Internationally set standards have a number ISO 9000. Items carrying this label indicate that the quality of the product is guaranteed.
   c. In Trinidad and Tobago the Bureau of Standards is the organisation that ensures that top quality products are exploited and that these products can compete with those on the international market.
3. **Outsourcing**
   Outsourcing is sometimes necessary for a firm to employ an outside firm to carry out either part of, or the entire, production process. The outside firm may provide a better quality output than the firm itself.

4. **Quality circles**

   a. Quality circles consist of a voluntary group of 5 to 15 workers who meet regularly to identify quality problems in the firm and to recommend possible solutions.

   b. The members are drawn from all levels of the firm; for example, shop floor workers, an engineer and a member of the sales department.

   c. The circles meet during the working day. A number of techniques are used to achieve the stated objectives; for example, brainstorming to develop new ideas and the random sampling of the firms output.

   d. The results of the quality circles meeting are presented to management who will implement the recommendations where necessary.

5. **Total quality management**

   a. Total quality management is a management culture that passes the responsibility for the quality of the firm's output to all workers.

   b. The main objective of total quality management (TQM) is to prevent defects.

   c. The objective is zero defects. This is achieved by using the right resources, production process and a well-motivated workforce.

   d. There is a special relationship between departments in the firm. One department supplies the input which another department (the internal customer) accepts. The internal customer will only accept this output if it meets the agreed standards. If it does not, it is sent back to the 'supplier' to improve the quality.

   e. Requirements for total quality management

   f. TQM will require in some cases drastic changes in the organisation. These may include:

      i. Training the workforce

      ii. Finding out the needs of the customers

      iii. Ensuring that suppliers are willing and able to supply high-quality inputs at all times.

      iv. Establishing quality control procedures.

      v. Specifying quality objectives.

      vi. Involving top managers.

6. **Kaizen**

   Improvements can be made in production, customer service, training methods, and internal communications

   a. **The Kaizen approach to quality**

      i. The Kaizen approach to quality is philosophy adopted by management whose objective is continuous improvement in all areas of the firm's operation.

      ii. In order to achieve their objectives, Kaizen groups are established and they meet on a regular basis to discuss problems and to find new ways of improving production and the level of productivity. Improvements are made on a small scale, so there is less likelihood that workers will lose focus.

      iii. It is not only concerned with production, it also involves improvements in customer service, training methods and internal communication. The main object is to improve quality.

      iv. It encourages workers to find new ways of improving the way the firm operates.

      v. The approach involves making small changes to improve quality. It is cost-effective and achieves its objective to improve quality on a continuous basis and for the firm to maintain its competitive edge.

   b. **Kaizen and the workplace**

      i. Kaizen, or continuous improvement, means that all workers should always be looking for ways to improve their productivity.

      ii. In order for there to be continuous improvement, training is vital. Training gives workers the necessary skills to perform their respective jobs in the firm and because workers have the necessary skills, the teams will work efficiently.

      iii. To achieve its objective, managers must view workers as being 'Theory Y' workers. That is, workers must be left to initiate ideas and management must give them the freedom to do so. Communication must be two-way: top-down from management to its workers and bottom-up from workers to management.

   c. **Limitations of Kaizen:**

      1. It is felt that over time Kaizen loses its value. This is so because it may be very difficult to find new ways of improving production as time passes.

      2. Where managers are likely to be more autocratic it may be difficult to implement Kaizen, as those managers may not want to give up their power and control in the organisation.

      3. Kaizen may be difficult to implement in firms where consumers taste change frequently, e.g. the fashion industry. The product life cycle is short; any improvements are normally made at the beginning of the production process.

# Lean production

1. **The objectives of lean production are to:**
   a. Reduce wastage: machines, labour, stock
   b. Improve labour productivity
   c. Increase capacity utilisation
   d. Improve quality
   e. Improve the level of motivation among workers.

2. **Lean production involves the use of Kaizen, Just-in-Time production technique and benchmarking.**

3. **The underlying philosophy of lean production is a partnership between management and workers. It can be difficult to create this partnership.**

4. **The firm benefits from lean production in the following ways:**
   a. Cost of production falls
   b. The quality of output will improve
   c. Workers will be more motivated
   d. Fewer accidents
   e. Less labour turnover
   f. Less absenteeism

5. **Benefits to customers**
   a. The customer will get a better quality product that means value for money.
   b. The firm is better able to cater to the needs of the consumers.

6. **Benefits to the economy**
   a. Resources are used more efficiently. Cost of production will fall. Selling price will fall.
   b. The effect on the domestic economy is tremendous:
      i. Demand for the firm's output will increase.
      ii. Employment levels will rise in the domestic economy.
      iii. If output is exported, the firm will be able to compete on the external markets.
      iv. The effect of this is an inflow of foreign exchange.
      v. It could also lead to an improvement in the balance of payments account.
      vi. There will be an inflow of foreign investment.
      vii. Increase in tax revenue for the government.
      viii. Finally, national income will rise and there will be an improvement in people's standard of living.

7. **Characteristics of lean production**
   a. Uses multi-skilled workers.
   b. The goal is to bring the operation as close as possible to perfection.
   c. It focuses on a 'pull system'.
   d. Produces volumes of goods.
   e. It uses less of everything in comparison with mass production.
   f. Uses machines that are flexible.
   g. Employees have a great deal of responsibility, which can motivate them. Sometimes it can create excess stress.

8. **Employees**
   a. Employees should be multi-skilled.
   b. They should be committed to producing goods and services of high quality.
   c. They should be flexible to respond to consumers demands.
   d. Employees must produce what consumers want and when they want it.
   e. It imposes heavy demands on management.
   f. It imposes responsibilities on shop floor workers who have to contribute to quality assurance schemes.
   g. Workers may need additional training as they adapt to quality circles and flexible ways of working.

9. **Training**
   a. For lean production to be successful, workers must be highly trained. Both workers and management will have new roles and responsibilities.
   b. Workers must be constantly looking for new ways to improve production.
   c. Lean production also requires the use of quality circles, job rotation and job enlargement. This means workers must be able to respond to any necessary change in the workplace.
   d. This means that workers must be well-trained to function efficiently in any area of the business. There must be continuous training for all workers.

10. **The link between lean production and inventory management**
    For lean production to be effective:
    a. Stocks must be supplied at the right price at the right time.
    b. Stocks are ordered when needed.
    c. There must be a close relationship with suppliers.
    d. The firm will hold zero buffer stock.

11. **The link between lean production and employees' role**

Employees play a key role in the success of lean production:

a. Employees must be motivated to work long hours.

b. They must have an input in decision-making.

c. They form Kaizen groups that meet regularly to discuss problems facing every department in the firm. It guarantees efficiency at every stage of production.

d. They offer possible solutions to existing problems.

e. Quality circles consist of employees who also meet with management to discuss work-related issues.

12. **The link between lean production and quality and capacity**

a. Lean production reduces the lead time between orders being made and delivered. Inputs are of a better quality.

b. Output is of a high quality due to the functioning of quality circles and Kaizen groups.

c. Production capacity will increase. The firm can produce more output with the same resources; wastage is reduced.

d. Management uses machines and the labour force to add value to the firm's output.

e. The objective is to be efficient in terms of zero defects and in terms of capacity utilisation.

 QUICK TEST

1. **State the dimensions of quality.**                                    **[5 marks]**

2. **Explain the importance of quality to a named firm.**                  **[15 marks]**

3. **Explain the concept of:**

   a. Quality control                                                      **[5 marks]**

   b. Quality assurance                                                    **[5 marks]**

# Productivity

## Objectives
At the end of this section you will know the:

1. **Difference between production and productivity**
2. **Factors that will increase productivity.**

## Productivity

1. **Productivity is a measurement of the efficiency with which a firm turns production inputs into output.**
2. **A rise in production is not necessarily a rise in productivity.**
3. **For example, if a 10 per cent increase in inputs results in a 10 per cent increase in output then what has increased is output; it is not an increase in productivity.**
4. **An increase in productivity occurs when the same inputs can produce more output in the same time.**
5. **It may also occur when the firm can use the same input to produce more output in a shorter time period.**
6. **Productivity is not the same as efficiency. Productivity measures the amount of input needed to produce a given level of output. Efficiency shows how well the input resources have been utilised.**
7. **Productivity is the relationship between the inputs a firms uses to produce a given product and the output obtained. It is therefore, the output per unit of input.**
8. **A rise in productivity occurs when the firm can increase output using the same inputs or producing the same level of output with fewer inputs or using less time to produce the given output.**
9. **Productivity is measured by the formula:**

$$\text{Productivity} = \frac{\text{Output}}{\text{Input}} \times 100\%$$

10. **Labour productivity measures output in terms of time taken to complete output.**
11. **Plant productivity measures the output in terms of machines output per hour.**
12. **Material Productivity measures output in terms of materials used.**
13. **Total productivity measures output in relation to all inputs.**

### Measuring productivity
There are various ways to measure productivity.

1. **Labour productivity:**
   a. This measures the output of labour over an agreed time period. It is measured by the formula.

   $$\text{Labour productivity} = \frac{\text{Output (per year)}}{\text{Number of employees}}$$

   b. Increases in labour productivity may be due to:
      i. Workers working harder
      ii. Better tools and equipment
      iii. Training
2. **Capital productivity**
   **This is measured by the formula:**

   $$\text{Capital productivity} = \frac{\text{Output (per year)}}{\text{Capital employed}}$$

### Factors that impact on productivity
1. **Technology**
   a. If the firm purchases new technology, e.g. fully automated equipment and workers have the skills to use this, then output will increase if the firm uses the same level of input.
   b. Technology reduces the time taken for a productive process to take place. In addition, it leads to a better quality product.
2. **Training**
   a. Workers must be given the necessary training to carry out their job. This is necessary to improve productivity. Training must be an ongoing process. If workers are multi-skilled they will be more motivated.
   b. A motivated worker is more reliable and punctual for work and has fewer accidents on the job. In addition, he or she can provide cover for any worker who is absent.

### 3. Market demand

If the market demand for a firm's output is greater than the supply of that output, and if inputs are in short supply, then the firm will have to find ways to increase its productivity.

Examples:

a. Employing better equipment – technology
b. Training and retraining workers
c. Reducing waste.

### 4. Competition

a. The level of competition in the market would force a firm to be more productive and to use the same resources to produce more output.
b. To survive in the market, prices must be low or lower than the existing market price for a similar product.
c. The greater the competition in the market, the greater is the need for firms to become more productive in order to survive.
d. Competition can also cause some firms to lower their prices in order to compete in the market, produce less and lower their productivity.

### 5. The quality of the labour supply

Basic qualities the labour supply must have in order to increase productivity include:

1. The labour force should be well-trained for the given tasks.
2. Workers should be motivated. Money motivates, according to Taylor, so a fair wage is essential; for other workers, a change to self-actualisation (Maslow).
3. Flexibility: willing to adapt to the changing internal and external environment.
4. Management must give workers the opportunity to express their creativity.
5. Workers must be healthy.
6. Workers must have positive work ethics.

---

 QUICK TEST

1. Define productivity. [5 marks]
2. Discuss the differences between production and productivity. [10 marks]

# Project management

## Objectives

At the end of this section, you will know:

1. **The value of the critical path method in managing a project.**
2. **How to construct a decision tree.**
3. **The limitations of decision trees and the critical path method to managers.**

In any business evaluation, time is vital. Time affects cost. Careful production planning can help to get a firm's new product to the market before its competitors can do so. This planning is therefore important. The critical path method provides some help here.

## The critical path method

1. **The critical path method is a technique used by managers to establish how a complex project can be completed in the shortest possible time frame.**
2. **It identifies the activities that must be completed on time to avoid delaying the whole project.**
3. **The critical path method ensures projects are finished on time, thereby reducing cost.**
4. **A 'network' will show:**
   a. The order in which each task must be undertaken
   b. How long each stage should take
   c. The earliest date at which the next stage can start.
5. **The network consists of two components:**
   a. An Activity: this requires time and resources. Activities are shown as arrows ($\rightarrow$) that run from left to right.
   b. A Node: This is the start or finish of an activity and is represented by a circle.
6. **All network diagrams start and end on a single Node.**
7. **When the manager has determined the length of time for an activity, it is possible to work backwards to find out when work must start.**
8. **The next stage is to identify when particular activities must start and finish. Therefore, it is important to number the Nodes which connect the activities.**
9. **The earliest start time (EST)**
   a. This shows the earliest times at which the following activities can be started. It lies at the top right-hand section of the Node.
   b. The EST provides two important pieces of information:
      i. The earliest date that resources will be needed, so cash will not be tied up in stock.
      ii. The earliest completion date for the whole project. This is the EST on the final Node.
10. **The latest finish time (LFT)**
    a. This show the time an activity must be completed. The time is recorded in the bottom right-hand section of the Nodes.
    b. The LFT shows the latest finish time of the preceding activities. LFT is calculated from right to left.

## 11. **The critical path**

  a.   It is made up of the activities which take longest to complete. They determine the length of the whole project.

  b.   These activities must NOT be delayed. If they are, the entire project will be late.

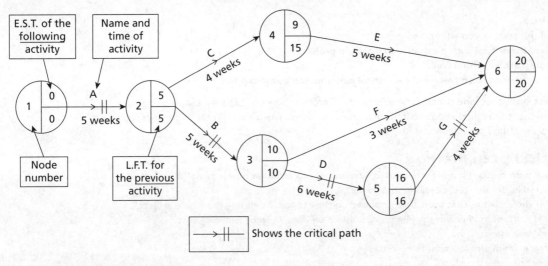

| | → ╫ | Shows the critical path |

## 12. **To identify the critical path:**

  a.   It will be on activities where the Node shows the EST and LFT to be the same.

  b.   It is the longest path through the Nodes.

  c.   The critical path is identified by drawing two short lines across the critical activities.

## 13. **Rules for drawing the network**

  a.   The network must start and end on a single Node.

  b.   No lines should cross each other.

  c.   Do not add the end Node straight away. See which activity follows first.

  d.   There must be no lines that are not Activity.

  e.   Draw the network with large circles and short lines as figures must be written in the Nodes.

## 14. **Pros and cons of critical path**

| Pros and cons of critical path | |
|---|---|
| **Pros** | **Cons** |
| › Time can be saved by operating certain activities simultaneously | › It may not be possible to represent complex activities |
| › It allows managers to make high-quality decisions | › It is based on estimates for the expected duration of the project. If the date is not correct, the whole project will be inaccurate |
| › Resources need to arrive Just-in-Time. Cost is reduced. It therefore improves the cash flow | |
| › It encourages managers to engage in detailed planning. This helps to reduce delays | |

# Decision trees

1.   **Decision trees are a common technique used by firms to reduce any uncertainty in their decision-making process.**

2.   **A decision tree is a schematic, tree-shaped diagram. It sets out options available to managers when making a decision.**

3.   **Decision trees are most often used when managers are faced with a problem that has more than one stage to it. In this type of problem, the outcome of one decision will have an influence on the next decision in a sequence. It helps managers to see the problem from a clearer angle.**

4.   **It shows the likely outcomes for a business of a number of courses of action, and the financial consequence of each action.**

5.   **By calculating the expected income and cost, managers can select the course of action providing the highest expected returns for the firm.**

## Points to remember

1. A decision tree is made up of **Nodes** and **branches**.
2. A square **Node** represents a point where a decision has to be made, i.e. **Square means Choices**. Circles represent chance events (probabilities).
3. Branches leading into decision **Nodes** do not have probabilities. All of the probabilities leading into an event **Node** must add up to 1 or 100%.
4. Expected monetary values are calculated by multiplying the actual value by the probability of the event occurring.
5. Evaluate the tree by working from the end of the branches to the start, i.e. from right to left.
6. At a decision **Node**, a square, the branch which best meets the desired outcome is selected.

| Advantages and limitations of decision trees as an analytical tool | |
|---|---|
| **Advantages** | **Limitations** |
| › It sets out problems clearly. It is a very useful tool in decision-making | › It may be difficult for managers to get meaningful data, which may not always be available |
| › It encourages a logical and quantitative approach to decision-making | › Making a strategic decision based purely on an analysis of one tree is not wise, especially if the data is not reliable |
| › It shows the expected values for each outcome | › It is costly in terms of time and money |
| › A decision tree diagram can be the centre of a management meeting | › The data is based on forecast and subjectively can encourage users to rely totally on the data |
| › Encourages better decision-making | › Does not take into account qualitative factors |
| › New ideas can emerge from the analytical processes | › It assumes a static set of circumstances |
| › Helps to take risks into account when making decisions | › Difficult to get accurate data relating to probabilities |
| › It is useful when accurate values can be attached to outcomes | › Any change in external/internal business environments will affect the accuracy of findings |

## Decision trees pre-analysis

1. In the calculations, start on the right and work backwards.
2. To get the expected values multiply outcomes by probabilities.
3. Add the expected values at each **Node**
4. Deduct any cost incurred
5. Use parallel lines to show the branches not taken

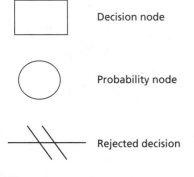

Decision node

Probability node

Rejected decision

 QUICK TEST

1. Discuss the importance of using decision trees as a project management tool.     **[10 marks]**
2. State the advantages of decision trees.     **[10 marks]**
3. Explain the steps in constructing a network diagram.     **[10 marks]**
4. Discuss the problems that exist when management use decision trees.     **[10 marks]**

## Key concepts

**Break-even output – Break-even point:** the level of output whose cost of sales is equal to sales revenue.

**Buffer stock:** this is the minimum of stock the firm should have to ensure a supply of stock is always available

**Contribution:** can be defined as the difference between sales revenue and variable costs of production.

**Economic order quantity (EOQ):** the ordering of quantity which minimises the balance of the cost of holding stocks and the re-order costs.

**Margin of safety:** shows how sales can fall before the business will make losses.

**Formulae:**

> Break-even point (in units) $= \dfrac{\text{Fixed cost}}{\text{Contribution per unit}}$

> Break-even point (in sales revenue) $= \dfrac{\text{Fixed cost}}{\text{Contribution per unit}} \times \text{Price per unit}$

> Level of sales (units) required to achieve target profit $= \dfrac{\text{Fixed cost + Target profit}}{\text{Contribution per unit}}$

> Margin of safety = Current output – Break-even output

> Profit = Margin of safety $\times$ Contribution per unit

# MULTIPLE CHOICE QUESTIONS

**1.** Which of the following is true about job production?
- I. It involves producing a good to cater to consumer specific needs
- II. It increases consumer satisfaction
- III. The firm does not benefit from economies of scale
- IV. It is usually undertaken by small firms
  - a. I, II
  - b. I, III
  - c. I, II, IV
  - d. I, II, III, IV

**2.** Which of the following are advantages of flow production?
- I. The firm can reap the benefits of economies of scale
- II. It allows for the standardisation of products
- III. It saves time. Workers do not have to move around the factory
- IV. The production process can be boring
  - a. I, II, IV
  - b. I, II
  - c. I, II, III
  - d. I, II, III, IV

**3.** In the product design, 'modularisation' means:
- a. Making items as cheap possible
- b. Making items as small as possible
- c. Making a model of the product first
- d. Producing products from inter-changeable sub-assemblies

**4.** 'Process layout' includes the following advantages except:
- I. Workers become more specialised
- II. Workers' productivity will increase
- III. It ensures high utilisation of machinery
- IV. There is not a continuous flow of work
  - a. I
  - b. I, II
  - c. I, II, III
  - d. I, II, IV

**5.** Capacity utilisation is important to a firm for all the following reasons except:
- I. The firm can gain the benefits of economy of scales
- II. The unit cost of production will fall
- III. It increases the firm profit margin
- IV. It enables the firm to purchase new equipment
  - a. I, III
  - b. I, II
  - c. I, IV
  - d. I, II, III

**6.** Value analysis can be defined as:
- I. A technique used by firms to evaluate the effectiveness of producing its output
- II. A technique used by firms to produce a product that caters to consumers need
- III. A technique aimed at reducing the cost of producing a product
- IV. A technique that adds to the cost of production
  - a. I, II
  - b. I, II, IV
  - c. I, IV
  - d. I, II, III

**7.** All of the following are forecasting techniques a firm can employ except:
- a. Salesforce composite
- b. Delphi method
- c. Consumer survey
- d. Demand and supply analysis

**8.** Work study involves an analysis of workers' task:
- a. To determine the most effective and efficient way of carrying out the task
- b. To study what has to be done
- c. To increase workers' output
- d. To compare output of workers in different departments

**9.** Labour productivity can be measured:
- a. In terms of output per man hour
- b. In terms of how productive labour is
- c. In terms of the output of the firm
- d. In terms of the number of workers employed in the firm

**10.** The advantages of using decision trees as an analytical tool are:
- I. It encourages better decision-making
- II. It shows the expected values of each outcome
- III. It sets out the problems clearly
- IV. It does not take into account qualitative factors
  - a. I, II
  - b. I, II, III
  - c. I, IV
  - d. I, II, III, IV

**11.** The use of critical path analysis has the following benefits for the firm:
- I. It saves time as some activities can be conducted simultaneously
- II. It allows managers to make high quality decisions
- III. It may not be possible to represent complex activities
- IV. It is based on estimates
  - a. I, II
  - b. I, III, IV
  - c. I, II, III
  - d. I, II, III, IV

**12.** The economic order quantity (EOQ) can be BEST defined as:
- a. The ordering of quantity which minimises the balance of cost of holding stock and the re-order cost
- b. The quantity of stock a firm must order
- c. The quantity of output a firm must produce
- d. The quantity of output a firm must produce based on its level of technology

**13.** The benefits of lean production to a firm:
- I. Cost of production falls
- II. Quality of output will improve
- III. Less labour turnover
- IV. Less absenteeism
  - a. I, II
  - b. I, III
  - c. I, II, III
  - d. I, II, III, IV

**14.** The following are techniques for improving quality:
- I. Bench-marking
- II. Quality circles
- III. Total quality management
- IV. The Delphi technique
- a. I, II
- b. I, II, III
- c. I, II, IV
- d. I, II, III, IV

**15.** The advantages of Just-In-Time stock control system includes:
- I. It reduces wastage
- II. There is more factory space
- III. The firm is less likely to experience a cash flow problem
- IV. It reduces the possibility of the firm benefitting from economies of scale
- a. I, II
- b. I, III, IV
- c. I, II, IV
- d. I, II, III, IV

**16.** A firm must control its stock levels:
- I. To control the amount of money held in stock
- II. To prevent wastage
- III. To prevent pilferage
- IV. To ensure the firm has an adequate level of stock for production
- a. I, II
- b. I, III
- c. I, III, IV
- d. I, II, III, IV

**17.** The following are assumptions of Break-even analysis except:
- I. All units of output are sold at the same price
- II. All units of output produces in the period are sold in that period
- III. There is no change in the variable cost of each unit of output produced
- IV. That fixed cost can change
- a. I, II
- b. I, II, IV
- c. I, II, III
- d. I, IV

**18.** Break-even analysis is an advantage to:
- a. Small and newly established firms
- b. The shareholders in the firm
- c. The consumers
- d. The government for tax purposes

# Unit 2
## Module 2

# Fundamentals of marketing

# The concept of marketing

## Objective

On completion of this section you will be able to define marketing and its related concepts.

1.  **The Chartered Institute of Marketing describes marketing as:**
    *The management process that identifies, anticipates and supplies customer requirements efficiently and profitably*
    **It therefore includes market research, product design, pricing advertising, sales promotion, customer service, distribution, packaging, warehousing and after-sales service.**

2.  **Exchange transactions**
    a.  This is an important concept in marketing; it facilitates the exchange of a good or service for money. In order for this exchange to take place there must be:
        i.   a meeting or communication between the buyer and seller
        ii.  at least two persons involved in the transaction
    b.  The person in this exchange transaction must have something they want to exchange, for example goods or services for the money.

3.  **Market: a market occurs wherever buyers and sellers come together to trade goods and services**

4.  **Value added:**
    a.  Value can be added to the product in the:
        i.   Production stages
        ii.  Marketing process
    b.  Value added is the difference between the cost of inputs used in production and the revenue the firms earn from the sale of the outputs. The inputs used in production would include raw materials, labour and components. Value added creates the surplus to pay, e.g. the wages, overheads and dividends.

# Implications of different marketing concepts

## Objective
On completion of this section you will be able to define different marketing concepts.

1. **The marketing concept**
   a. The marketing concept involves conducting market research to ensure that what is produced is based on the market research of the firm.
2. **The product concept**
   a. The product concept implies that the firm's objective is to produce a high-quality good with the belief that consumers will purchase it.
   b. The concept is employed by the business, the belief is that, if the product is superior to its competitors, consumers will demand the product.
   c. One implication of this concept is that it may not place sufficient emphasis on market demand. This could mean that once launched, the product may fail to achieve its target.
3. **The production concept**
   a. The production concept is based on the belief that if a product is made it will be sold.
   b. The production concept is based on the assumption that the producers know what consumers will demand.
   c. One advantage of this concept is that in large-scale production the unit cost of production and selling price will fall and profits will increase.
   d. An implication is that there is limited choice and no market research, only technical research into product design and there is little advertising.
4. **The selling concept**
   a. The main focus here is to sell the product. The business will invest heavily in advertising and sales promotion.
   b. This concept is used when:
      i. The firm has to sell new products
      ii. Stock must be sold to improve the cash flow
      iii. The stocks are becoming obsolete.
   c. More emphasis is placed on what the business has to sell and not on consumers' demand.
5. **The societal marketing concept**
   a. This is a much wider marketing concept and it focuses on the business profit, consumers, other stakeholders and the business's social responsibility.
   b. An advantage of this concept is that the business is perceived to be carrying out its social responsibility. This, it is believed, would increase demand for the business output.
   c. The business would still aim to satisfy consumers' demand more efficiently than the competition in the market and, at the same time, fulfill its social responsibility.
   d. The problem here is that the business's cost of production could increase.

 QUICK TEST

Define the following:
1. **Markets**                                                    [8 marks]
2. **Value added**                                               [8 marks]
3. **Product concept**                                           [8 marks]
4. **Production concept**                                        [8 marks]
5. **Societal marketing concept**                                [8 marks]

# The marketing environment

## Objectives

On completion of this section you will know:

1. **The variables in the microenvironment.**
2. **How to analyse the effect of the macro environment on the operation of a business.**

The marketing environment can be divided into the microenvironment and the macro environment.

## The microenvironment

The microenvironment consists of all other firms, organisations and individuals that contribute to the success of the firm. These include:

a. Company suppliers: they provide the necessary inputs for production; e.g. in a bakery the supplier is the firm that supplies eggs.

b. Competitors: competition is present in a market economy. Firms must therefore be able to compete and gain market share in order to survive. A number of strategies can be employed, e.g. cheaper prices, better terms and condition of sale, better quality product.

c. Customers: they purchase the firm's product.

d. The media flow: the media views of the business can impact on its profitability.

e. All firms and organisations that, in anyway, can affect the business.

f. Marketing intermediaries: external consultants the firm can use in a bid to gain a competitive edge in the market. They include marketing and advertising consultants, who provide information to firms in relation to all marketing data, e.g:

   i.  Promotion of the firm's output

   ii.  Distribution of the product

   iii.  Selling of the product

## The macro environment

This is the external environment. Unlike the microenvironment, the firm has no control over the macro environment. The macro environment consists of:

a. Demographic factors: examples include age and gender; as the population ages, firms must make the necessary adjustments to cater to an aging population, e.g. changing styles and materials used in the production of shoes.

b. Environmental natural factors: in the production and marketing of its output, the firm must attempt to preserve the natural environment.

c. Economic factors: if the economy is in a boom, consumers will demand more expensive goods and services. Producers will therefore increase output. If there is a downturn in the economy, output will contract.

d. Political factors: government policies have a direct impact on the operation and profitability of a firm; e.g. the implementation of a minimum wage will increase the cost of production and in the long-run lead to the firm substituting machinery for labour. Other political factors include health and safety regulations, pollution control policies.

e. Cultural factors: these are factors associated with the 'way of life' of consumers. Cultural factors will indicate to producers what consumers demand.

f. Trade unions: these can affect the operations of a business in terms of the demands they make, for example increased wages for workers. They could begin to put pressure on management, if management wants to replace workers with technology.

g. Ethical issues: firms must consider ethical issues. They must make every attempt to reduce their level of pollution and must not produce products that are harmful to consumers.

 QUICK TEST

1. **State the composition of the microenvironment.**                    [8 marks]
2. **State the composition of the macro environment.**                    [8 marks]

# Marketing research

## Objectives

On completion of this section you will know the:

1. **Importance of market research.**
2. **Benefits and limitations of market research.**
3. **Stages of market research.**

1. **The role and importance of market research**

   Marketing Research is: *'the collection, analysis and communication of information, undertaken to assist decision-making in marketing'* (Wilson, A. 2003)

2. **Why is marketing research important?**

   Marketing research is important for the following reasons:

   a. Communication: the communication gap has widened, so there is a need for more information to make better decisions on what should be produced.

   b. Competition: competition has increased, so there is a greater need for more detailed knowledge about what competitors are doing.

   c. Technology: there is a need for information, in order to detect changes in technology and be able to react well and survive.

   d. Taste: there are changes in tastes and purchasing habits, so there is a need for more information in order that improved processes can be put in place.

   e. Cost: information needs to be obtained because if this is insufficient, marketing costs would be high and may exceed the cost of production.

3. **The benefits of market research**

   Market research:

   a. Aids top decision-making: firms can make a better decision, for example, in terms of pricing and distribution of its output.

   b. Defines the size of markets.

   c. Provides a link with the outside world: it provides information on the trends in the market and a guide to further action.

   d. Reduces the risk of possible failure as businesses can be more aware of market demand.

   e. Improves public relations: as consumers views are taken into account.

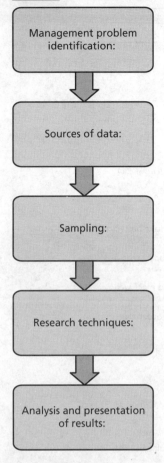

> **Define problem**
>   o Information required
>   o Why?
> › **Type of research to be carried out**
> › **Should relate to the problem identified**
> › **Clearly state objectives and identify**

> › **Primary data collection:**
>   o Surveys, experiments, observation
> › **Secondary data collection:**
>   o Magazines, journals, newspapers

> › **Probability sampling**
> › **Non-probability sampling**

> › **Focus groups**
> › **Surveys**
> › **In-depth interviews**
> › **Observation**

> › **Tables**
> › **Pie charts**
> › **Line graphs**
> › **Bar charts**
> › **Pictograms**

Stages of market research

**4. Presentation of results**

There are a number of different techniques to present the findings from the firm's market research. They are:

a. Pie charts: useful to show proportions. There is a limit to the number of items that can be included

Pie chart

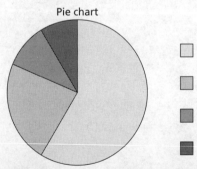

b. Bar graphs: they use bars of standard width, but varying length to show comparisons of data, over time. They facilitate comparisons because they are clear; however, only straightforward data can be shown.

Bar graph

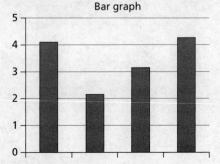

c. Frequency curves

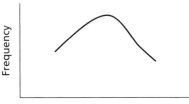

d. Tabulation

| Column 1 | Column 2 |
|----------|----------|
| 2.3 | 4.7 |
| 1.5 | 6.4 |

Tabulation

e. Histograms/ line graphs: represent a frequency distribution, i.e., the area of the block is proportional to the value of the variable measured. It gives a sense of continuity, which is absent in the bar chart.

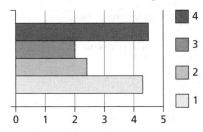

Histogram/line graph

f. Pictograms: use pictures to represent data. The impact is usually strong and only simple and limited data can be shown.

Pictogram

## 5. Limitations of market research

It is important to note that firms should not depend entirely on the findings of their market research for the following reasons:

a. The sample size may be too small and not representative of the potential market.

b. The firm may lack the financial resources to achieve a more accurate account of the market.

c. The firm may need to know the results of the market research quickly, so a more detailed research is not feasible.

d. If it is to identify a market, the time taken for the research and the time the product arrives on the market may be too long. Competitors may have entered the market.

e. The questionnaire may have leading questions, or the interviewer may project their own point of view, or the interviewee may not answer the questions truthfully.

f. Competitors' actions and/or responses were unexpected.

g. A sudden change in tastes and fashion occurs.

h. Market research is like looking in the rear view mirror. It does not fully indicate where the firm is going.

 QUICK TEST

1. **State the importance of market research.** [8 marks]
2. **Explain the limitations of market research.** [8 marks]
3. **List the stages of market research.** [8 marks]

# Principles of market segmentation

## Objectives

On completion of this section, you will:

1. **Know the importance of segmentation.**
2. **Know the bases of segmentation.**
3. **Assess consumer buying behaviour.**

1. **The importance of segmentation**
    a. It assists the firm to identify unfilled market segments and to create products to cater for these segments
    b. It allows the firm to structure its marketing techniques to cater for the specific segment. Advertising a product for children will be different from marketing a product for senior citizens.
    c. It will lead to increased profits for the firms, as production and marketing of the product will be specific to that market segment.
    d. Firms can dominate the segment and, over time, gain monopoly power.
    e. It allows firms to cater to various market segments by making slight alterations to a given product; e.g. cakes for vegetarians and non-vegetarians.
    f. It allows the firms to direct the marketing budgets to those segments that will give the firm the highest return.

2. **Target marketing**
    a. Target marketing is that part of a market, i.e., the specific segment to which the firm aims to sell its products, e.g housewives.
    b. The choice of the target market will determine how the firm distributes its product, e.g., house-to-house or at supermarkets. It will also determine the price charged for the product.

3. **Mass marketing**
    a. Mass marketing is a marketing concept that involves appealing to the whole market, not just a segment in the market. It involves the use of television, newspapers or website.
    b. Some advantages of mass marketing include:
        i. The entire market is targeted.
        ii. The firm benefits from economies of scale as output is increased and cost of production falls.
        iii. Risks are spread over the entire market.
        iv. Profit margins will increase.

4. **Niche marketing**
    a. Niche marketing is a corporate strategy based on identifying and satisfying small segments of a larger market.
    b. It allows small firms to operate successfully alongside large firms. It also allows specialist firms to develop.

| Advantages and disadvantages of niche marketing ||
|---|---|
| Advantages | Disadvantages |
| › The first firm to identify that there is an unfilled market segment can produce a product to fill this existing niche | › Niche marketing is marketing a product or service for a small segment of the market. It means therefore that it may be difficult to spread its fixed cost over a sufficiently large volume of sales to gain a large profit margin |
| › Since it is the first to produce the product, e.g. ice cream for vegetarians, it will become established in the market, a position it will maintain even in the face of competition | › Demand for products in niche markets often declines in a recession. The firm therefore will incur high costs |
| › Firms selling in a niche market can sometimes charge a high price for their product | |
| › The firm can focus the needs of consumers in these segments and gain market share. It allows small firms to identify and to sell its products to this niche, and may therefore avoid competition from larger firms | |

6. **Market segmentation**
    a. This involves analysing a market to identify types of consumers in the market.
    b. By matching the different types of consumers to the products on the market, the firm will be able to identify unfilled market niches.

7. **Basis of segmentation**
   a. Demographic: this involves dividing consumers on the basis of:
      i. Age: e.g. different styles of watches for different age groups
      ii. Gender: items of clothing for females will be different to those designed for males
      iii. Social class: this classifies consumers according to income levels, occupation or level of education
      iv. Religion: this is particularly important for firms producing foods: e.g. Hindus would not consume beef.
   b. Geographic: this involves segmenting the market according to regions.
      i. It involves producing output that consumers, in that geographic region, will demand.
      ii. If the firm is selling its products, e.g., to Muslim countries, the firm will not include, in its product, any extract or designs of the pig.
      iii. If the market segment is Hindu, the product will not contain beef.
      iv. Cotton may be the fabric of choice for garments for the tropics; for colder temperatures, warmer fabric will be used.
   c. Behavioural: this classifies people according to their values, interests, opinions and personality. It seeks to determine the lifestyles of consumers and then tailor their products to meet the demands of the specific group of consumers.

8. **Consumer buying process**
   The main objective of all firms is to produce a product that consumers will demand. Consumers go through a series of stages before making a decision to demand a product . These stages are as follows:
   a. Recognition: the consumer recognises that they need the product, e.g., food, or they will be able to purchase an item such as a washing machine, at a sale price.
   b. Researching: the consumer then begins their own market research to determine where the item is cheaper; for example, websites or local stores.
   c. Refining and reflecting: the consumer looks at alternatives and begins to form an opinion that would be cost-effective.
   d. Other viewpoints: if the purchase is an expensive one, the consumer may get the opinion of other consumers, and any additional information available.
   e. Decision: the consumer is now in a position to make a decision on whether to purchase the item and where.
   f. Purchase: the item is then bought.
   g. Evaluation: Does the item satisfy the consumer? Is it working well? Does it fulfill the terms and conditions of purchase? For example, after-sales services.

9. **The purchasing process**
   In order to ensure that consumers will demand their product, producers have to ensure that the production department and marketing department meet consumers' demand. These are the steps that can be followed:
   a. Easy recognition: convey to consumers the benefits and strengths of the product.
   b. Researching: use market research to establish the strengths of the product over its competitors.
   c. Refining and reflecting: point out to consumers why they should purchase your product (e.g. better guarantee and after-sales service).
   d. Branding: this helps to sell the product.
   e. Purchasing: make the actual purchase of the item easy (e.g. discount for cash purchase).
   f. After purchase: create in the mind of the consumer that you value them.
   g. Review: where possible, maintain contact with the customer, in order to ensure that the consumer is satisfied with the purchase.

---

 QUICK TEST

1. **Define market segmentation.**                                               **[8 marks]**
2. **Define the concept of:**
   a. Niche marketing                                                            **[8 marks]**
   b. Target marketing                                                           **[8 marks]**
   c. Mass marketing.                                                            **[8 marks]**

# Product management

## Objectives

On completion of this section, you will:

1. **Understand the product life cycle (PLC).**
2. **Know the value of the production life cycle to marketing managers.**

### 1. The product life cycle

This is a theory that states, all products go through stages that can be compared to human beings.

A product, like humans passes through the following stages:

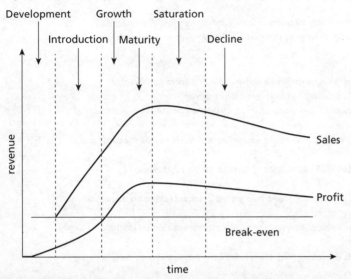

The classical PLC

| Product life cycle stages, cash flows and marketing activities associated with them | | | |
|---|---|---|---|
| | **Stages** | **Cash Flows** | **Marketing Activities** |
| **1** **Development** | › Research and development › High cost › Marketing strategy identified | Cash is flowing out of the business. Money has to be spent on: › Research and development › Market research › Product design | |
| **2** **Introduction** | The product is launched. › Sales are low, as some consumers are not aware of the presence of the product on the market › The firm has to invest heavily in advertising the product to gain market share › The risk for the firm is high if the product is entering a competitive market, where there are well established producers; there may be no guarantee for the success of the product › The product is unlikely to be profitable at this stage. Cost of production in addition to advertising cost may be greater than the revenue obtained from the sales of the product | › Cash outflow very high | › There is a high cost of advertising to inform and persuade consumers to purchase the product. The firm may also have to use market penetration pricing to increase consumer demand |

| | Stages | Cash Flows | Marketing Activities |
|---|---|---|---|
| **3** **Growth** | › The firm's advertising cost has increased the demand for the firm's output. This has resulted in the growth of the firm. It means therefore that the firm can benefit from economies of scale<br>› Economics of scale means the cost of production would fall. Cost per unit of output falls. Selling price falls. Demand for the product increases. As prices fall, market share increases. Profits increases. The benefits to the firm of selling the product are greater than the cost of production | › There is increased cost as the firm attempts to expand output. Sales begin to increase as consumers become aware of the product. This is because of increased advertising. Growth is taking place | › As sales begin to increase and other firms are attracted to enter the industry, it will be necessary for the firm to continue to allocate revenue to advertise their product to ensure market share<br>› It will also be necessary for the firm to use sales promotion strategies. This is necessary to maintain customer loyalty before the entry of competitors |
| **4** **Maturity** | › At this stage most consumers have already purchased the product<br>› Sales, therefore, are growing but very slowly | › The firm is using advertising and sales promotion to maintain market share<br>› The firm may use extension strategies to attract new consumers who are loyal to their product. For example, the firm may give out free offers<br>› Cash continues to flow into the firm | › As the product reaches the maturity phase, the firm may attempt to change its packaging in a bid to market its product<br>› The firm may also attempt to use its marketing strategy to attract new customers from other firms in the industry |
| **5** **Saturation** | › At this stage sales are falling even more | › The saturation phase is a continuation of the maturity phase of the product<br>› The major difference here is that the market becomes saturated. This means sales level off and so too does the revenue to the firm | |
| **6** **Decline** | › The demand for the firm's output falls<br>› This means the profit falls<br>› Consumers may buy substitutable products<br>› The firm now may consider removing the product from the market | › In this stage of the PLC, sales of the product are falling<br>› To deal with this, the firm has three options:<br>  o Use marketing strategies to recapture its market share<br>  o Reduce its losses by cutting its cost<br>  o Take the product off the market<br>› The cost of production is greater than revenue obtained from the sale of products | › The firm attempts to cut costs. Not much is spent on advertising, because the firm may be considering taking the product off the market |

| | Stages | Cash Flows | Marketing Activities |
|---|---|---|---|
| **7**<br>**Elimination** | › The firm may decide to take the product off the market if it is believed that it would be impossible for the product to regain its former position in the market | | |
| **8**<br>**Extension** | If the firm believes that the decline in sales is temporary then the firm may decide to extend the life of the product through a number of strategies.<br>› The firm may change the product slightly, e.g. adding nutrients to foods, e.g. Vitamin C to hamburgers<br>› The firm may change the packaging to make it more attractive and functional for consumers, e.g. plastic bottles replacing glass bottles<br>› The firm may decide to engage in door-to-door selling to attract a different market segment<br>› The firm may find a new use for an old product | | |

2. **Usefulness of PLC**
   a. PLC can be a useful analytical model to assist business decisions.
   b. It can give an insight regarding the markets in which the firms operate. This information will be beneficial to firms as they make marketing decisions.

3. **Limitations of PLC**
   a. The theory lacks precision. It is difficult to determine where the product is at any point in time.
   b. When will the product enter the next stage? This is difficult to determine.

4. **Alternative PLC**
   a. It must be noted just as in the life of a human, not everyone will live to become old.
   b. Products, too, can only enter the market for a short period and, for a variety of reasons, the manufacturer may withdraw the product from the market.

5. **Straw on Fire PLC**
   a. These are products that enter the market and gain popularity through intensive advertising and sales promotion.
   b. The sales decline as consumers are attracted to another product that they are now persuaded to purchase; for example, children's toys.

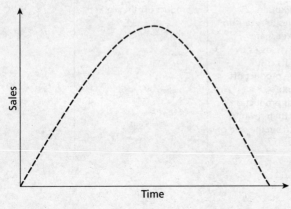

Straw on Fire PLC

**6. Flop PLC**
   a. A product that enters the market and consumers fail to purchase can be described as a Flop product.
   b. The demand for these products simply did not exist.
   c. The reason for this could be because of ineffective market research, advertising or sales promotion.

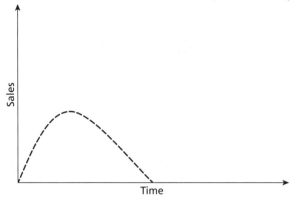

Flop PLC

**7. A comparison of Straw on Fire and Flop PLCs**

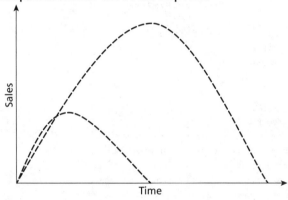

Comparison of Straw on Fire and Flop PLCs

**8. The leapfrog PLC**
   a. This type of PLC can be seen in a market where firms that are large and powerful compete for market share and consequently market dominance.
   b. In such a situation, one firm may leapfrog the other to gain market share. To achieve this, the firm may change the design of the product to make it more appealing to consumers. This will translate into increased sales, market share and increased profits.
   c. Rival firms in the industry, in an effort to regain market share, will leapfrog and change their design. The end result is that sales, market share and profit in the other firm will decline.

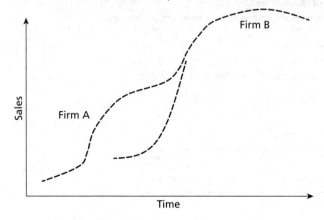

Leapfrog PLC

9. **The long cycle PLC**
   a. There are some products that enter the market and continue to experience increased demand.
   b. This may be due to intensive market research, advertising and sales promotion.

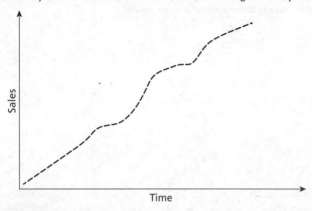

The Long Cycle PLC

10. **Factors affecting the length of a PLC**
   a. Fashion: Fashionable items will have a shorter life cycle as fashion changes rapidly to make way for the next fashion.
   b. Technology: Changes in technology can make a product obsolete in a short period of time.
   c. Durability: Products that are durable will normally have a longer PLC.

11. **As a product reaches its decline stages, the firm has one of two options**
   a. Implement extension strategies.
   b. Withdraw the product.

12. **Extension strategies**
   There are a number of extension strategies that the firm can implement:
   a. Change the appearance of the packaging of the product, for example change the colour. The colour of the package for the Dairy Dairy Milk powder in Trinidad and Tobago was changed from blue to green. This was done with the objective of gaining an increase in demand for the product.
   b. Market the product to different segments in the market. For example, baby lotions essentially produced to cater for babies are now marketed to older people, as the advertisement points out for the baby in each of us.
   c. Change the way the product is marketed, e.g. selling online.
   d. Change the channel of distribution, e.g. using a shorter or longer channel of distribution.
   e. This will depend on the nature of the product and the location of the markets.

## The Boston Matrix

1. **Marketing managers have a number of tools they can use when they are planning their product mix and strategy. The Boston Matrix is one of these strategies.**
2. **It is a way of analysing a PLC.**
3. **The Boston Matrix shows how the product portfolio of a business can be seen in relation to the contribution it can make to the present or future of the business.**
4. **It therefore allows the business to classify their products according to how they are growing in the market.**
5. **The Boston Matrix puts products into four categories:**
   a. Problem Child or Question Mark or Wildcat Products
      i. These are products that have a small share of the market and will therefore need a lot of financing, e.g., marketing, for these products to reach their full potential.
      ii. All new products will start from this box.
   b. Star Products
      i. Products that are successful will move to become star products
      ii. Here the product has gained market share and there is tremendous potential for growth
   c. Cash Cows
      i. These are products that have a large market share. However, the product is growing slowly.
      ii. These Cash Cow products bring in revenue for the firm. This revenue is used to finance the development of new products.
   d. Dogs
      i. Products that fall into this group have a low market share. They are products that are in decline. It is unlikely that there will be any growth in demand for them.

ii.  Dogs are products for which the cost of production is greater than the revenue obtained from their sales. They will be taken off the market.

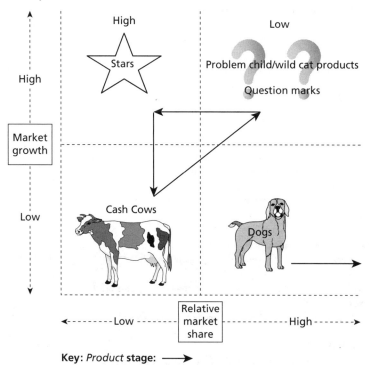

Boston Matrix diagram

6.  **The value of the Boston Matrix to managers**
    a.  It is an important technique that allows mangers to determine their strategy as it relates to the development of new products.
    b.  It is valuable for managers to know their product range so they can identify the strengths and weaknesses of their products.
    c.  It can serve as a tool to forecast the position of the firm's output in the future and to develop strategies for marketing. The strategies may include:
        i.  Put policies in place to maintain the firm's position in the market, e.g. increase marketing.
        ii.  Put policies in place to gain a better market position, e.g. intensive advertising.
        iii.  Put policies in place to get the most profit in the short-run, e.g. sales promotion
        iv.  Take the loss, taking the product off the market.
    d.  Managers should know to avoid having too many products in any single category.
7.  **Continuing the production of Cash Cows will provide profit to develop newer products. The benefits of producing these products will be greater that the cost of developing and promoting others.**
8.  **Problem Children products are needed as they could become the future Cash Cows of the business.**

## The dimensions of the product mix

1.  **The product mix simply refers to the fact that the firm is marketing more than one product. In fact it is marketing a mixture of products.**
2.  **A firm's product mix can be classified as:**
    a.  Deep
    b.  Wide
3.  **A deep product mix**
    a.  The product mix is classified as deep if the firm is marketing a number of products within each product line; for example, the local bakery may offer its customers a variety of cakes that could include vegetarian cakes, non-vegetarian cakes, chocolate cakes, fruit cakes, sponge cakes, marble cakes or coconut cakes.
    b.  In fact, it offers almost any kind of cakes that customers would demand. This is an advantage to the firm as it caters to all segments in the market.
    c.  The objective is that market share would increase. The firm's profit would increase.

4. **A wide product line**
   a. A wide product line means that the firm is offering consumers a wide variety of products
   b. For example the local corner store may offer its customers a wide variety of products; for example, food items, kitchen equipment, garden supplies.
   c. This means that the firm is a one stop shop. The objective is to satisfy consumers' needs so that they remain loyal to a particular firm.
   d. It saves consumers time in shopping and it increases the firm's market share and profits.

5. **Product line**
   A product line consists of a group of products closely related to each other in the following ways.
   a. They are in about the same price range.
   b. They may have a common distribution channel.
   c. There may have a common customer group.
   d. The use for which the product is used may be similar; for example, the product line for the health-conscious consumer may overlap with those product lines focused on a gourmet food experience.

6. **Product extension**
   Product extension occurs where a firm, in order to maintain its market share and to attract a new market segment, may become mired in product extension strategies.
   a. The up market stetch:
      i. The firm can alter its products to attract customers in higher income group;
      ii. For example, a fashion designer may use more expensive fabric when making a garment.
   b. The down market stretch:
      i. Here the firm attempts to create a demand for its garments from customers in the lower income bracket; for example, using a less expensive fabric to produce the same style garment.
      ii. The firm can also modify the garment to customers who may demand a slightly different garment.

## New product development process

1. **In order to maintain its market share and, by extension, its profitability it is crucial for firms to develop new products.**
2. **Every product goes through its own life cycle, but very few would remain in the maturity phase of the PLC indefinitely.**
3. **It is therefore necessary for the firm to replace these products with new ones.**
4. **Classification of a new product**
   A new product can be classified as:
   a. An existing product that the firm has changed drastically so that the consumers view it as new.
   b. A totally new product that is different from any product the firm currently produces.
   c. An existing product that has been slightly changed so that consumers perceive it as new. The product is new and indeed different from any existing product of the firm.

### Stages in the development of a new product

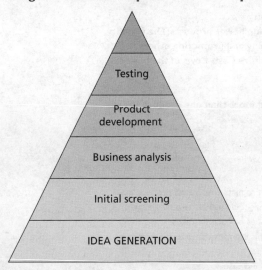

Stages in the Development of a new product

Once the firm has decided it has to produce a new product, it will follow the stages set out below.

1. **Idea generation**

   The development of a new product begins with an idea. Ideas cost nothing. There are a number of techniques that the firm can use to generate ideas for its new product.

   a. Through its market research, gaps in the market can be identified and the firm can develop new products to fill these gaps.

   b. Through brain storming: here the firm decides what it believes that consumers need. Then the product is produced. Then through advertising and sales promotion the firm creates the demand for the product.

   c. Analysing competitors' products. Firms may do research into their competitors' products and gain a new insight into what to produce. The firm, too, can use its own product as a basis for the development of a new product.

   d. Ideas for the new product can also be generated from the firm's market research. In addition, ideas may come from consumers, retailers, wholesalers as well as the salesforce.

2. **Screening**

   a. Before an idea is developed into a product, the firm will have to determine if the benefits of developing and marketing the product would be greater than the cost of producing this new product.

   b. The firm therefore has to predict how marketable and profitable the product will be. This process is referred to as the screening process.

   c. During the screening process, the firm will get answers to vital questions, such as:

      i. Would the product be demanded by consumers?

      ii. Does the firm have the financial resources to produce the product?

      iii. Does the firm have the necessary personnel to develop the product?

      iv. Can the production department produce the product?

      v. Does the marketing department have the resources to market the product?

      vi. Is the product compatible with the existing range of products the firm is producing

      vii. Does the uniqueness of the product guarantee consumers' demand?

   d. It is only when the idea has passed the initial screening process that the firm will see the viability of producing the product. If it is viable then the firm will allocate the necessary funding required to develop the product.

3. **Business analysis**

   › Product ideas that pass the initial screening tests are then taken through another series of analyses. Here the producer will want to find out if the demand for the sale of the product will be sufficient to make the introduction of this new product viable.

4. **The development phase**

   a. During this phase, ideas that have the potential to be translated into consumers' demand will be settled.

   b. Personnel from different parts of the firm are involved, e.g. production and finance.

   c. In this phase of the development of the new product emphasis is placed on the design of the product

   d. In the design process, the functional aspect of the product is emphasised. Does the product, e.g. a vacuum cleaner, work? Does it perform all the services it is designed to perform? Does it meet customer satisfaction?

   e. Then there is the formal design of the product. What would the final product look like? Would it be attractive to consumers?

   f. In developing a new product, e.g. a vacuum cleaner, functionality and aesthetics must be combined. Consensus will demand a product if it satisfies the intended purpose for which it is bought and at the same time has aesthetic value.

   g. This will involve the firm using value analysis to get the desired result at a lower cost.

   h. Factors influencing the design of a product

      i. Operation: It is easy to operate

      ii. Reliability: It is reliable

      iii. Safety: It is safe to use

      iv. Maintenance: It is easy to maintain

      v. Legally sound: Are all legal requirements observed, e.g. types of materials used, paints etc.?

      vi. Environmental impact: Is the product environmentally friendly?

      vii. Meeting market needs: Does the product design fulfill market requirements?

      viii. Alignment to company image: Is the design in keeping with the company image?

5. **Testing**

   a. This allows the firm to evaluate marketing strategies. It allows the firm to forecast future sales of the product. After the design stage has been completed a small quantity of the product is put on the market to test its feasibility.

   b. The market testing will give the firm the opportunity to understand what will happen when the product is finally placed on the market.

   c. It also allows the firm to adjust its marketing mix; for example, the price, place, product and promotions may become evident at this stage.

d. Remember at this stage:
  i.   The product is in its most acceptable form
  ii.  The price of the product has been established
  iii. The packaging has been decided
  iv.  The methods of advertising have been determined
  v.   The sales force has been briefed on all that is required to launch a successful new product on the market.
  vi.  The results of the test marketing will be evaluated.
  vii. If successful at this stage, the production department will begin production.

6.  **Commercialisation and launch**
  a. At this stage all potential problems in launching the product have been resolved.
  b. The firm finally launches the new product on the market.

## Factors that limit the development of new products

1. **Lack of financial resources**
Most firms may lack the financial resources that are necessary for the development of the new products.

2. **Lack of human resources**
In addition, most firms may lack the human resources that are necessary for the development of new products

3. **The consumer market**
  a. In any given market there is a percentage of that market that will not readily demand a new product that enters the market. This means it will take time before consumers feel comfortable enough to demand the product.
  b. Firms therefore will be reluctant to produce a new product. It is more likely that the firm may alter an existing product to create the perception that it is new.

4. **Legal constraints**
  a. In order for a firm to successfully launch a new product, that product must satisfy the legal requirements of the country.
  b. For example, Bureau of Standards, FDA (Food and Drug Administration) must give their approval.

5. **Technology**
  a. This is costly to install, service and replace.
  b. Firms therefore may be reluctant to purchase technology where this is needed for the production of new products.

 QUICK TEST

1. **Describe in detail the various stages of the classical product life cycle.**  [15 marks]
2. **With the aid of diagrams, explain two other product life cycles.**  [10 marks]
3. **Describe the marketing strategies a firm can use at each phase of the product life cycle.**  [10 marks]
4. **Explain the usefulness of the product life cycle to marketing managers.**  [15 marks]
5. **State the limitations of the product life cycle to marketing managers.**  [10 marks]
6. **What characteristics of market share and market growth might be displayed by:**
  a. Question Mark or Problem Child or Wildcat?  [5 marks]
  b. Cash Cow?  [5 marks]
  c. Dog?  [5 marks]
  d. Rising Star?  [5 marks]
7. **When a product is in decline, what are the options available for the marketing manager? Give reasons for your answer.**  [10 marks]
8. **Draw and label a diagram of a classical product life cycle and discuss.**  [10 marks]

# Pricing decisions

## Objectives

On completion of this section, you will know:

1. **The various pricing strategies a firm can employ.**
2. **How to analyse the effect of the various pricing strategies on the profitability of the firm.**
3. **The factors influencing pricing.**
4. **How to assess the role and importance of pricing.**

## Pricing decision

Price is the value placed on a product by a business. This value is expressed in terms of money that consumers must pay in order to obtain the product. The pricing decision a firm makes is based on the objectives of the firm and the external environment in which the firm operates.

### The objectives of pricing

i.  **The objectives of firms in the public sector may differ from the objectives of firms in the private sector. Firms in the private sector may have the following objectives:**

1.  Profit maximisation: firms in the private sector will have their main objective in the long-run to maximise profit. This occurs when the cost of producing an additional unit of output is equal to the revenue obtained from its sale.
2.  Sales revenue maximisation: firms may set a price to maximise sales revenue.
3.  Increase market share: firms may want to increase market share by selling output at a lower cost than it obtains in the market. They may sacrifice short-term profits for long-term gains.
4.  A target level of profits: the firm will establish a level of profit it requires. The target is set in monetary terms, or as a percentage of capital employed.
5.  Profit margin: the firm will set the price to maximise its profit margin. Prices are high, as the firm is based on the assumption that high income earners will purchase the item.
6.  Survival: in the short-run, firms would have survival as their main objective.

ii.  **One of the reasons why firms are interested in their demand curve is that it enables them to calculate the total revenue that will accrue to them at any given time.**

Total revenue = Price × Quantity demanded

## Factors influencing pricing decisions

The following factors influence the firms pricing decisions:

1.  **Changes in income:**
    a.  A normal good is one where the demand will increase as income increases. If income falls, demand would also fall. An increase in consumers' real income, with supply of goods and services remaining the same, will cause prices to rise.
    b.  If supply increases to match the increase in income, prices could remain unchanged.
    c.  In the long-run, supply can increase as the firm gains the benefits of economies of scale and prices will fall.
2.  **Demand for the product:**
    a.  The quantity demanded for a given product will determine its price, if all other variables affecting demand remains unchanged.
    b.  If demand increases then prices will rise and if demand falls, prices will fall.

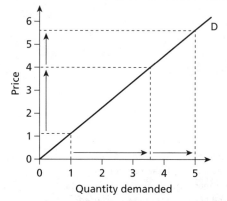

Diagram showing how an increase in price affects the demand for the product

3. **Consumer preference:**
   a. There are a number of factors that affect consumers' preference; e.g. the level of advertising, the price of other goods.
   b. If the supply of potatoes remains the same in the short-run and consumers are demanding more, then the price of potatoes will increase. If supply remains the same and the demand falls, prices will fall.

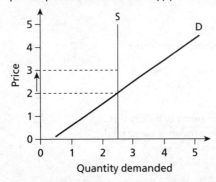

Diagram showing how an increase in price affects the consumers' preference

4. **Cross elasticity:**
   a. This is measured by the formula:

   $$\frac{\text{Percentage change in quantity demanded of Good X}}{\text{Percentage change in quantity demanded of Good Y}}$$

   $$\boxed{\frac{\%\Delta Dx}{\%\Delta Dy}}$$

   b. Goods which are substitutes have a positive cross elasticity; for example, if the price of butter increases, consumers would demand less butter and more of its substitute, margarine.
   c. Goods which are complements have a negative cross elasticity. An increase in the price of film, will lead to a fall in demand for cameras.

5. **Elasticity of demand:**
   › **Price Elasticity of Demand – Measures how Demand is affected by a change in Price.**
   › **Income Elasticity of Demand – Measures how Demand is affected by a change in Income.**
   › **Cross Elasticity of Demand – Measures how Demand is affected by a change in the Price of another good.**
   a. This measures how demand is affected by a change in the price of a good, a change in consumers' income, or a change in the price of another good.
   Formula for Price Elasticity of Demand

   $$\frac{\text{Percentage change in demand}}{\text{Percentage change in price}}$$

   $$\boxed{\frac{\%\Delta D}{\%\Delta P}}$$

   b. If the good is elastic, a fall in price of 2 per cent will cause total revenue to increase by more than 2 per cent.
   c. Price elasticity is measured by the formula:

   $$\frac{\text{Percentage change in quantity demanded}}{\text{Percentage change in income}}$$

   $$\boxed{\frac{\%\Delta Qd}{\%\Delta y}}$$

   d. A percentage raise in income can lead to a greater percentage change in quantity demanded. Then, as income rises, producers can keep prices constant and total revenue will increase.

## Pricing strategies

The following are examples of pricing strategies a firm can employ:

a. **Cost-plus pricing:**
   i. This is a pricing policy adopted by firms that are innovators in the market. Firstly, add its fixed cost and variable cost, and then divide the total cost by the number of units produced. This gives the firm the average cost of production. To this figure, add its mark-up. This is the final price the consumers must pay.
   ii. Disadvantages: (1) they do not take into account the external environment; and (2) products can be overpriced.

b. **Competition pricing:**
   i. Competition in the market will determine the price the firm will charge for its product.
   ii. A monopoly market: it is the price maker. Prices will be higher than in a competitive market.
   iii. If there is competition in the market, a number of different pricing strategies can be used (e.g. loss leaders).
   iv. Firms can set a price that is comparable to rival firms in the market.
   v. If there is competition in the market, firms can offer their products at a lower price than the market.

c. **Perceived value:**
   i. Market research will establish consumers' perception of the value of the product.
   ii. Consumers will be willing to pay more for a product if they believe they are getting value for their money. If the price is higher than its competitors, the product will be marketed as a product of superior quality.

d. **Going rate:**
   The firm sets a price based on other prices in the market; here the products are homogenous and therefore there is competition.

e. **Penetration pricing:**
   i. This pricing policy can be used by new firms entering a competitive market.
   ii. The firm sets a price below the ruling market price.
   iii. In order to gain market share, the firm will invest in advertising and sales promotion and, in the long-run, the firm will increase prices.
   iv. Sometimes the product can also be sold below the cost of production, in the short-run.

f. **Price skimming:**
   i. In this pricing strategy the firm sets it prices high in order to attract trend-setters or the very rich.
   ii. The firm will keep the same price in the long-run, or reduce its price when competition enters the market.
   iii. Price skimming is done by firms as they launch new products, e.g. those that are technologically advanced, such as cell phones or pharmaceuticals.
   iv. A high introductory price gives the consumer the perception that the product is high value. In this way, it allows the firm to reduce the price in the long-run and gain market share.

g. **Marginal cost pricing/ Contribution pricing:**
   i. This method of pricing is based on the firm using its variable cost or marginal cost of production to establish the price of its output.
   ii. It is normally used when output levels are changing.
   iii. In the short-run, only variable costs will change.
   iv. The variable cost, when covered, any extra price the firm charges will go towards the fixed cost.
   v. Marginal cost pricing is therefore also referred to as contribution cost pricing.
   vi. If competition exists in the market, the firm may need to reduce its price to increase the demand for its product.
   vii. This, however, can only be done in the short-run.

h. **Loss leader pricing:**
   i. Here the firm sets a price at a loss.
   ii. This is a method of sales promotion.
   iii. It is believed that consumers will be attracted to the low-cost item in the store, purchase the item as well as other items.
   iv. This will cover the loss sustained in the low-price item.

i. **Predatory pricing:**
   i. Established by firms that are well established in the market.
   ii. Financial resources to sell products below cost of production.
   iii. They do so to remove any competition in the market.

j. **Price discrimination:**
   i. Normally practiced by monopolies.
   ii. It sells its products in two different markets at two different prices.
   iii. In one market, demand is elastic; the firm may therefore set a lower price in order to compete.
   iv. In the other market, demand is inelastic, e.g.: a monopoly.

k. **Mark-up pricing:**
   i. Determined by the retailer.
   ii. Retailers purchase goods from wholesalers, and then add their own percentage mark-up to establish the selling price.
   iii. Sometimes this percentage mark-up is suggested by the wholesaler.

l. **Full cost or absorption cost / pricing:**
   This occurs where the firm determines the unit cost of production and then adds an agreed profit margin.

**m. Price variation:**

Firms may alter its price to maintain market share if:

i.   A customer is paying in cash.

ii.  A customer is buying large quantities.

iii. They are a loyal customer.

**n. Special offer pricing:**

In this pricing strategy, the firm will reduce the prices of its products for a given period of time, e.g. cell phones at Christmas.

**o. Psychological pricing:**

In this pricing strategy, the firm would set a price at, for example, $8.99 instead of $9.00, or $29.99 instead of $30.00.

---

 QUICK TEST

1. **State the factors influencing pricing decisions.**                    **[8 marks]**
2. **State the importance of pricing.**                                    **[8 marks]**
3. **State the pricing strategies a firm could use.**                      **[8 marks]**

# Distribution management

## Objectives

At the end of this section, you will:

1. **Know the various routes a product can take.**
2. **Discuss the principles of distribution.**

**a. Role of distribution in an organisation**

The role of distribution in an organisation is to get the right product, to the right consumer, at the right time, in a way which is most convenient.

**b. Factors influencing distribution decision**

An efficient channel of distribution will enable a firm to make its output available to customers when required at the lowest cost to the firm. The channel the firm uses could be long or short. The factors the firm will consider are as follows:

1. The product: is it perishable; does it have a high unit cost; is it custom built; is it expensive to handle and bulky? Producers selling large quantities of low price goods are more likely to use a short channel.
   Services: are sold directly through a short channel. Goods are more likely to be sold indirectly.
2. The market: if the demand for the good is urgent, the firm will use a short channel. If the market is geographically dispersed, the firm may use an indirect channel.
3. Control: if the producer wants to have control over the quality of the product, it is likely that a short channel will be used. Where control is not an issue, for example: selling low cost items, longer channels may be employed.
4. The company: large companies may have the resources to distribute their products themselves. They may be able to open their own retail department if the demand for their product is high. Smaller firms would tend to employ a more indirect route.

**c. Types of distribution channels**

1. Distribution channels can be classified as:
   i. Intensive: if there are many intermediaries
   ii. Selective: if there are a small number of intermediaries
   iii. Exclusive: if there is one intermediary
2. In order to get the product to the final consumer, distribution involves: the manufacturer, agent, wholesaler and retailer.
3. The firm can use various ways to deliver goods to consumers to meet their demand.

   **Route 1:** From manufacturer to consumer.

   **Route 2:** From the manufacturer, to wholesaler, to retailers, to final consumers.

   **Route 3:** From manufacturer, to retailer, to consumer. Large retailers can now buy in bulk and therefore there is no need for the wholesaler.

   **Route 4:** From manufacturer, to agent, to consumer. This route is used by car manufacturers. The agent represents the manufacturer. The agent will be representative of the repetitive market.

   **Route 5:** From manufacturer, to agent, to retailer, to consumer. The route is employed by: For example; large supermarkets importing supplies.

**d. Logistics strategy**

1. Marketing logistics is involved in planning, implementing and controlling the physical flow of materials, final goods and related information from the point of origin to meeting consumer requirements at a profit.

2. Logistics is concerned with the movement and storage of goods. Its objective is to place the right goods, at the right place, at the right time, at the right cost and in the right condition to the final consumer.

3. These are the five 'rights' identified by Professor Collin Bramford.

**e. Types of distribution strategies**

1. Intensive distribution strategy:

   This is a strategy used by firms that distribute their output to a large number of sales outlets. These firms therefore will achieve the maximum coverage of the market. Firms employing intensive distribution have the following characteristics:

   i.   They cater for low income groups

   ii.  Their objective is mass marketing

   iii. They have adequate capacity for expansion

   iv.  They enjoy economies of scale

   v.   The products sold do not require much help from sales persons

2. Selective distribution strategy:

   This involves making the product available through a selected number of outlets. Selective distribution will be employed, where:

   i.   The producer wishes to have control over the intermediaries.

   ii.  The producer is better able to provide training on how to distribute the products.

   iii. There is a less likelihood that the item will be returned.

   iv.  Intensive distribution would result in conflict between the various intermediaries.

---

 QUICK TEST

1. **Why is distribution important to a business?**  [10 marks]

2. **What factors influence a firm's distribution decisions?**  [15 marks]

# Promotion strategy

## Objectives

At the end of this section, you will know the:

1. **Objectives of promotion.**
2. **Tools of promotion and their advantages.**

a. **The objectives of promotion**

Firms promote their products to:

i. Compete with other firms in order to maintain their position in the market.

ii. Introduce their products to a new market.

iii. Enhance their corporate image and thereby promote their whole range of products.

iv. Improve the image of the firm. This will be necessary if consumers have a negative perception of the firm.

v. Inform consumers about the product, and to persuade them to purchase it.

vi. Increase the demand for the product at various stages of the PLC.

b. **Tools of promotion**

i. Advertising

Advertising is a promotional activity involving one-way, paid for, communication from producer to potential consumers.

| Advantages and disadvantages of Advertising | |
|---|---|
| **Advantages** | **Disadvantages** |
| › It informs the consumer | › Cost of advertising is high and this cost is passed on to the consumer in the form of higher prices |
| › It helps the firm to differentiate its product from others | › The money spent to advertise could have been spent on, for example, research and development |
| › It can assist the firm to have a steady demand for its product | › It creates confusion in the mind of the consumer, who now finds it difficult to make a correct choice |
| › It helps to reduce sales fluctuations | › Persuasive advertising may cause consumers to purchase unnecessary items |
| › It gives the firm a competitive edge | › The benefits of economies are not passed on to the consumer |
| › It allows the firm to benefit from economies of scale. Unit cost of production falls, selling prices fall, demand increases and there are greater profits for the firm | › The information often misleads the consumer |
| › It is cheaper than other forms of advertising because it reaches a wider market segment | › Consumers may purchase items they do not need |

ii. Personal selling

This is a marketing strategy that is employed in the marketing of expensive products by well-trained sales staff; for example, cars and electronic equipment.

| Advantages and disadvantages of personal selling | |
|---|---|
| **Advantages** | **Disadvanatges** |
| › The sales staff are well-trained, they understand each consumer and can tailor their marketing to cater for each one, to guarantee sales | › It demands a well-trained sales staff. This can be very expensive |
| › The firm can gain valuable feedback from consumers about the product through the sales representatives | › Staff turnover is high. This is an added cost that must be frequently borne by the firm |

iii. Sales promotion:

| Advantages and disadvantages of sales promotion | |
|---|---|
| **Advantages** | **Disadvantages** |
| › It can increase sales. It could persuade customers to sample a product for which they may not have budgeted. | › When the promotion stops, sales can decline |
| › It can increase market share | › It can create the perception that the product is not top quality |
| › It provides the firm with feedback | |
| › It can aid a firm as it launches a new product on the market or as an extension strategy to increase sales and extend the PLC | |

v. Publicity

| Advantages and disadvantages of publicity | |
|---|---|
| **Advantages** | **Disadvantages** |
| Positive publicity will: | Bad publicity could have a negative effect on the: |
| › Increase demand for the products | › Reputation of the company |
| › Act as a valuable forum to introduce new products. | › Demand for the products |
| › Increase market share | › Any new products the firm may produce |

 QUICK TEST

1. **State the objectives of promotion.**      **[10 marks]**
2. **State the differences between advertising and sales promotion.**      **[10 marks]**
3. **State the advantages and disadvantages of personal selling.**      **[15 marks]**

# Internet marketing

## Objectives
At the end of this section, you will know the:

1. Opportunities created by internet marketing
2. Challenges of internet marketing

## Opportunities created by internet marketing
Internet marketing provides opportunities for both the consumer and producer.

### Benefits to producers who use the internet to market their products
1. The market for the product can be spread over a large geographic area.
2. The cost of renting a location to market their products is eliminated. In urban areas this cost could be very high.
3. There is the opportunity to give more information about the product.
4. Cost of advertising is lower, after the initial cost is covered.
5. The producer does not have to look for customers; the consumers look for the producer.

### Opportunities for consumers created by internet marketing
1. Consumers pay less for the products. This is because the producer's cost is also lowered.
2. Consumers can browse the site wherever they are located.
3. Consumers have the opportunity to do their own market research before making their decision to purchase.
4. Items purchased can be delivered at their home. This is particularly valuable for consumers, who, for any given reason, cannot leave their home to go shopping.
5. Consumers can return the product if they are not satisfied.

### Challenges of internet marketing
1. Payment: consumers may not want to give their credit card or debit cards details, for the fear that people will hack into their account.
2. Retailers: they may experience difficulty in getting their product sold if their supplier decides to market the product online.
3. Terms and conditions of purchase: consumers would want a speedy delivery of items purchased. This could be a challenge for suppliers who may not have the necessary infrastructure to achieve this. Consumers will also want the condition to return items if not satisfied.
4. Getting a website: this has a high initial cost and is a particular challenge for small businesses.
5. Information: the company can obtain a lot of information about customers' buying behaviour. The challenge here is to establish a system to use this information.
6. Culture: businesses trading online must look at the cultural differences of their potential market. This will determine how web pages must be designed to be effective.

### Importance of e-commerce to business organisations
1. It is a cheaper way to market the firm's output over a larger geographic area.
2. It increases the firm's market share.
3. Business transactions can be easily carried out as payments can be made online.
4. There is no time barrier for consumer shopping. It therefore increases the demand for the firm's output.
5. It reduces the delivery time.
6. It is important for firms to keep the competitive edge in order to retain their share of the market, as other firms may be using this media.
7. The visual presence of the product online can influence impulse buying, as firms engage in persuasive advertising.
8. It encourages firms to be more efficient in order to maintain market share. This is so, because consumers can make comparisons with other products on the market.

9. It allows firms to source cheaper raw inputs.

10. It saves the firm time, as business can be conducted at anytime.

11. It reduces costs in terms of management and other personal travelling expenditure the firm is likely to incur.

 QUICK TEST

1. Explain the importance of e-commerce to Caribbean businesses.            [15 marks]
2. What are the challenges that Caribbean businesses face by internet marketing?            [15 marks]
3. List the opportunities created by internet marketing for Caribbean businesses.            [15 marks]

# Key concepts

**Exchange transaction:** this is the exchange of goods and services, for payment, usually in the form of money.

**Marketing:** a marketing process that identifies, anticipates and supplies what the customers demand; it includes market research, product design, pricing, advertising, promotion, customer service, distribution, packaging and after-sales service.

**Market orientation:** used by firms which place consumers' demand at the centre of its decision-making.

**Marketing strategy:** the strategy used by the firm to achieve its marketing objectives.

**Market penetration:** a firm's policy to increase sales volume.

**Markets:** a place where buyers and sellers come together to exchange goods and services. E.g. street market, the stock market and capital market.

**Market segmentation:** a strategy to analyse a market to identify the different types of consumers. Markets might be segmented according to similarities, demographically, psychologically and geographically.

**Market share:** the percentage of total revenue of sales accruing to a firm in a given market.

**Primary data:** information which does not exist and is collected through the use of interviews, questionnaires, surveys, etc.

**Product life cycle:** this is a theory describing the stages a product passes through during its existence in the market.

**Product mix:** a number of products a firm is marketing.

**Product orientation:** used by a firm which places the focus on the production process.

**Sales force:** a team of sales representatives, employed by the firm to achieve a more efficient distribution of its products, wholesale and retail outlets, or to sell directly to customers.

**Sales promotion:** the use of short-term incentives to increase the demand for the firm's product, e.g. free offers, competitions.

**Secondary data:** information which has been collected previously. It is used by another researcher for a purpose for which it was not originally collected.

**Telemarketing:** contacting customers via telephone in order to persuade them to purchase the firm's product.

**Test marketing:** the launch of a new or improved product within a small defined area in order to measure its sales potential.

**Value added:** the difference between revenue earned by the firm and the cost of production, e.g. raw material, overheads.

## Questions

1. a. Define the concept: 'marketing'. [3 marks]
   b. State the factors that influence the choice of a channel of distribution. [11 marks]
   c. Discuss the advantages and disadvantages, to the firm, of using
      intermediary channels. [11 marks]
2. a. Explain what is meant by each of the following:
      i.   Branding
      ii.  Price penetration
      iii. Price skimming
      iv.  Distribution channels [12 marks]
   b. Discuss the advantages and disadvantage of each of the above concepts. [13 marks]
3. a. Define the concept: 'market research'. [5 marks]
   b. State the importance of market research to the firm. [10 marks]
   c. Discuss the limitations of market research. [15 marks]
4. a. Distinguish between market segmentation, niche marketing and
      mass marketing. [10 marks]
   b. State the benefits of mass marketing to a firm. [5 marks]
   c. Discuss the benefits and limitations of market segmentation to a named firm. [10 marks]
5. a. Draw a diagram of a typical product life cycle. [5 marks]
   b. Explain how each stage of the product life cycle will affect the:
      i.   Production department
      ii.  Finance department
      iii. Marketing department. [15 marks]
   c. State the limitations, to a firm, of using the product life cycle. [5 marks]

# MULTIPLE CHOICE QUESTIONS

1. Market research is beneficial to a firm for all the following reasons except:
   a. It aids in decision-making
   b. It improves communication for faster decision-making
   c. It defines the size of the market
   d. Government will know how much to tax the firm

2. The microenvironment consists of all of the following except:
   a. Customers
   b. Competitors
   c. Government
   d. Suppliers

3. Which of the following is a macro-environmental marketing factor?
   a. Consumers
   b. Suppliers
   c. Government
   d. Economic factors

4. Penetration pricing strategy refers to the strategy of:
   a. A firm entering a new market
   b. Reducing the price of a product to attract in a competitive market
   c. Conforming to the established price in the market
   d. Pricing a product based on the full cost of the product

5. A segment of the population selected to represent the population as a whole is called:
   a. A survey
   b. A sample
   c. Market segment
   d. Market research

6. The pricing method that is based on the consumer's point of view with regards to the value of the product is known as:
   a. Break-even pricing
   b. Going-rate pricing
   c. Value-based pricing
   d. Contribution-cost pricing

7. The Delphi technique is a form of subjective long-range forecasting that relies on:
   a. The use of expert panels achieving consensus
   b. It relies on market forces to determine demand and supply
   c. Data provided by retailers
   d. Consumers' surveys

8. A product-oriented firm has the following characteristics except:
   a. It is efficient
   b. Cost of production is low
   c. It responds to consumer needs
   d. It produces a high quality product and expects that consumers will buy it

9. Cross subsidisation means:
   a. Substituting one product for another
   b. Using the profits from some products to compensate for the losses sustained in other products
   c. Two products to be sold at a reduced cost
   d. Obtaining financial help from the government to cover the losses sustained

10. The extension strategies a firm can use to rejuvenate a product, include all of the following except:
    a. Changes in the product
    b. Changes in the packaging
    c. Changes in the method of distribution
    d. Increase the price of the product

11. When a firm uses price skimming to establish its selling price, it means that:
    a. The firm is using a variety of prices to sell its products
    b. Pricing a new product with such a high price that it is only purchased by trend-setters
    c. Prices are low to compete with existing firms on the market
    d. Consumers who purchase the products will get a discount

12. When a firm is price discriminating, this means that:
    a. It is charging different prices to different consumers for the same product
    b. All consumers must pay the same price
    c. The quality of the product determines the price
    d. The firm charges a different price for the different products sold

13. Services are said to possess the following characteristics, except:
    a. Intangible
    b. Perishable
    c. Inseparable
    d. Accountable

14. In the Boston Matrix, 'a Cash Cow' product is that product that has:
    a. A large market share in a high growth market
    b. A large share of a declining market
    c. A small share of the market in a low growth market
    d. A small market share in a high growth market

15. E-commerce is best defined as the use of the internet for:
    a. Conducting market research
    b. Advertising the firm's products
    c. Buying and selling
    d. Establishing social connections

16. The term 'Loss Leader' means:
    a. The product is not needed by consumers
    b. The product has been replaced by another product
    c. A product is sold below cost of production
    d. A leader who has lost the ability to lead

**17.** Which of the following is not a qualitative factor affecting location?

   a. Infrastructure
   b. Environmental factors
   c. Management preference
   d. Labour cost

**18.** Which of the following is NOT a forecasting technique?

   a. Consumer surveys
   b. Jury of experts
   c. The Delphi method
   d. Cost/ Benefit

**19.** The following factors limit the development of new products except:

   I. Lack of financial resources
   II. Lack of human resources
   III. Legal constraints
   IV. Lack of technology

   a. I, II, IV
   b. I, II
   c. I, II, III
   d. I, II, III, IV

**20.** Which of the following best describe the stages or life cycle of a normal product?

   a. Introduction, growth, saturation, maturity, decline
   b. Introduction, growth, maturity, saturation, decline
   c. Introduction, maturity, growth, decline
   d. Introduction, saturation, decline, growth

# Unit 2
## Module 3

# Small business management

## Learning Objectives

Upon completion of this revision module, you will:

1. **Know the nature and characteristics of entrepreneurship**
2. **Know the relationship between different business organisations**
3. **Know the criteria for measuring size of firms**
4. **Know the challenges faced by small businesses**
5. **Know the opportunities that exist for small businesses**
6. **Know the type of assistance given to small businesses**
7. **Know how to construct a business plan**

## Introduction

Businesses stay small for the following reasons:

1. **The owner's objective is to remain small:**
   › This will give closer contacts with consumers.
   › They will be able to control staff better.
   › There will be additional responsibilities as the firm grows.
   › Possibly the fear of diseconomies of scale.
2. **The market size:**
   › If the market size is small, businesses are likely to remain small, e.g. in rural areas.
   › If the firm is producing highly specialised products, e.g. expensive handmade jewellery.
3. **The type of industry:**
   **Most firms will remain small, e.g. auto repair shop, hairdresser.**
4. **Barriers to growth:**
   **Small firms may be unable to break down barriers established by larger firms in the market, so they remain small and cater for a small market.**
5. **Financial problems:**
   › It may be difficult to obtain the necessary finance for growth and expansion because:
      o Firms may not have the necessary collateral.
      o The rate of interest is too high.
      o Other avenues for raising capital are not cost-effective.

# Nature and characteristics of entrepreneurship

## Objectives

At the end of this section, you will know:

1. **Corporate entrepreneurship**
2. **Social entrepreneurship**
3. **Successful entrepreneurship**
4. **How management can foster the spirit of entrepreneurship.**

### a. The entrepreneur

1. The International Labour Organisation (ILO 1987) defines the 'Entrepreneur' as people who have the ability to see and evaluate business opportunities; to gather the necessary resources to take advantage of them; and to initiate appropriate action to ensure success.
2. An entrepreneur is an action-oriented highly motivated person who sees and makes the most of opportunities that other individuals do not see.

### b. Corporate entrepreneurship

1. The term 'entrepreneurship' can be used to describe the qualities of an individual who is flexible; exhibits imagination; is willing to take risks and to be innovative.
2. Such individuals can be an asset to the organisation and management should create an environment in which they can flourish.
3. In order for entrepreneurial abilities to further develop, management must give entrepreneurs the freedom to try out new ideas and to take risks.
4. Management should place entrepreneurs in positions where they can become involved in innovative training.
5. Management must be willing to listen to ideas that entrepreneurs put forward.
6. Management must emphasise that entrepreneurship within an organisation is highly valued.
7. Management must listen to ideas that may be presented to them:
   a. It is important to note that some ideas will not be accepted, yet management must encourage the development of new ideas.
   b. Management must implement creative ideas quickly. This will motivate workers and encourage the creation of new ideas
   c. Management must put in place an avenue for the collection of new ideas, e.g. a suggestion box placed in a convenient place for workers to place their suggestion.

### c. Social enterprise

1. A social enterprise can be described as an organisation that has been set up to cater to the needs of the society.
2. These organisations obtain the revenue needed for their operations from donations and the various commercial activities they organise during the year.
3. Their main objective is to improve the society and the environment in which they operate.
4. **The goals of a social enterprise:**
   The main objective of a social enterprise is to enable society to function better by assisting members in the society who are deprived in some way.

### d. The characteristics of successful entrepreneurs

1. The characteristics of an entrepreneur depend on the nature of the enterprise with which they are involved
2. Someone who establishes a social enterprise will focus all their attention on creating a better social environment. Another entrepreneur, for example one who establishes a business, will have profit maximisation as their prime focus.
3. **Characteristics of an entrepreneur:**
   a. A risk taker: willing to take calculated risk and to have the confidence he or she will be successful.
   b. Goal-oriented: sets their goal and combines the factors of production to achieve this, so they are therefore very focused and profit-oriented.
   c. Persistent: optimistic individual who has the confidence that regardless of the situation, they will never give up.
   d. Flexible: has the ability to react quickly to changes in the external environment, e.g., a change in the rate of interest.
   e. Innovative: constantly developing new ideas.
   f. Creative: finds a new way of doing things and is open-minded and resourceful.
   g. Sociable: able to relate to the people around them.
   h. Hardworking: has the capacity to work for long hours, committed to the task at hand.
   i. Moves past failure: has the capacity to deal with failure, i.e., to never give up.
   j. Good communication skills: has a good command of language. Ability to communicate with groups and individuals easily and to get along with others.

**e. How can management foster the spirit of entrepreneurship?**

1. Management can provide workers with the resources necessary to develop their ideas.
2. Management style should be more democratic. This means having open communication with workers and then giving them the forum to develop new ideas.
3. Motivating workers so that they are comfortable to voice their ideas, while reminding them that not all their ideas could be entertained by the firm.

---

 QUICK TEST

1. **Define the following concepts:**
   a. Entrepreneurship                                                    [3 marks]
   b. Social Entrepreneurship                                             [3 marks]
   c. Corporative Entrepreneurship                                        [3 marks]
2. **State the characteristics of an entrepreneur**                       [10 marks]
3. **What can the management of a manufacturing firm do to encourage an entrepreneurial spirit?**                                                   [10 marks]
4. **What can prevent the development of an entrepreneurial spirit in a manufacturing firm?**                                                       [10 marks]
5. **What is the government of your country doing to foster the development of entrepreneurs in your country?**                                      [8 marks]

# Business and economic systems

## Objectives

At the end of this section, you will know:

1. **The characteristics of the following economic systems in which businesses operate:**
   a. Free economy
   b. Mixed economy
   c. Planned economy
2. **How the various economic systems affect decision-making.**

## Economic systems in which businesses operate

### i. The free economy

1. The major business decisions are made by entrepreneurs in the private sector and there is no public sector.
2. Entrepreneurs decide what to produce, how to produce, when to produce and for whom to produce.
3. Demand and supply factors interact to create an equilibrium in the market.
4. If the firm is a monopoly, the producer is 'king' and the firm is the price maker.
5. The monopolist determines the price for his output, the quantity to be supplied.
6. The objective of each business decision it to maximise profits.

### ii. The mixed economy

**Business decisions are made by:**

1) The public sector
2) The private sector

1) **The public sector:**
   a. Pure public goods: the government will provide those goods and services that the private sector will not provide. This is because these cannot be sold as there is no way of excluding those who did not pay for the goods and services from consuming them.
   b. Merit goods: the government will also provide those goods and services which can be provided by the private sector, but at a high price, e.g. education, health care.
   c. Government also can influence the business decision made by firms in the private sector by passing laws that can impact on their decision-making, e.g. the minimum wage, health and safety regulations and laws governing the location of businesses.

2) **The private sector:**
   a. Firms here are free to make any decision: what to produce? when to produce it? how to produce it? for whom to produce it?; but that decision must be in accordance with government regulations and control?
   b. Monopolies, in this sector, can maximise profits, but not at the expense of the consumers.
   c. Government (e.g. of Trinidad & Tobago) has established the Restricted Industries Commission (RIC) that controls the activities of monopolies in this sector.
   d. The Bureau of Standards establishes standards for products.
   e. Laws passed by the Government of Trinidad & Tobago that affect business decisions, e.g. health and safety regulations, minimum wage, location, affect the operations of firms in this sector.
   f. Firms in this sector, main objective is to maximise profits.

### iii. The planned economy

   a. Decision-making is the responsibility of the state.
   b. The state makes all business decisions in the interest of the public's welfare.
   c. The state decides: what to produce, when to produce, how much to produce, for whom to produce.
   d. There is no private sector.

### iv. Advantages and disadvantages of free, mixed and planned economies

1. **A free economy: advantages and disadvantages**

| Advantages and disadvantages of a free economy ||
|---|---|
| **Advantages** | **Disadvantages** |
| › There is no government intervention | › There is unequal distribution of income |
| › There is consumer sovereignty in the market | › Wasteful competition exist |
| › Consumers maximise satisfaction, producers maximise profits and the owners of the factors of production would maximise the returns for each factor | › Essential services are not adequately produced |

| | |
|---|---|
| › There is freedom of choice for consumers, producers and those who own the factors of production | › Important services: pure public goods will not be produced<br>› Merit goods: will be produced in limited quantities at high prices |
| › Competition among firms forces prices down | › Monopolies that exploit consumers will exist |
| › The market forces determines price | › Public welfare will not be maximised because of high social cost |
| › The factors of production are more efficiently used | |
| › New and more efficient methods will be developed as producers aim to maximise profits | |

2. **The mixed economy: advantages**
   › The public sector and private sector co-exist.
   › Efficient use of resources.
   › There is freedom in the private sector to make economic decisions (what to produce, how to produce it and for whom), but that decision is subject to the government's regulation.
   › There is a more equitable distribution of income now, in the free market economies.
   › Government can pass laws to protect the environment.
   › A wider variety of goods are provided.
   › The government provides what the market will not provide, i.e. pure public goods, because a price cannot be placed on the good; and merit goods, which are goods that the private sector will produce only in limited quantities but goods that are vital for the welfare of citizens.

   The advantages of the mixed economy are essentially the advantages of the free enterprise market economy and the centrally planned economy

3. **Planned economy: advantages and disadvantages:**

| Advantages and disadvantages of a planned economy | |
|---|---|
| **Advantages** | **Disadvantages** |
| › There is economic stability as the state controls and plans | › There is a loss of consumer sovereignty |
| › Wasteful competition does not exist in the market | › There is a disincentive to work and innovate |
| › Production and the allocation of resources are efficient as the government is better able to allocate resources efficiently | › It is difficult to predict consumers' demand |
| › Wages are determined by the state, so there is less inequality of income | › Bureaucracy and red tape |
| › The welfare of citizens is maximised | |

 QUICK TEST

1. **State the various economic systems that exist.** [5 marks]
2. **Who makes the decisions in a mixed economic system?** [10 marks]
3. **What is the role of the government in a mixed economic system?** [10 marks]
4. **Give examples of how government can influence the activities of small businesses.** [10 marks]

# Size and growth of business

## Objectives

At the end of this section, you will know:

1. **The criteria used for measuring the size and growth of firms**
2. **The definition of a small firm**
3. **The advantages and disadvantages of small firms in relation to large firms**

## Introduction

There are difficulties in measuring the size of a firm. Many different indicators are used, but none can be regarded as precise on its own

### a. Criteria for measuring size of a firm

i. **Output**

   1. Output is the method used to measure the size of firms in the same industry.
   2. Output is easy to measure.
   3. It gives the necessary data on the firm's ability to benefit from bulk buying and reap the benefits of economies of scale.
   4. The limitation of this method of measuring size of the firm is that:
      i. High output does not necessarily mean the firm is large.
      ii. A firm employing few people and low levels of output, but selling its output at a high price, will be considered as large.

ii. **Labour force**

   1. This can give a general idea of the size of the firm.
   2. It is difficult to use this measure when comparing sizes of firms in different industries.
   3. It will be higher in service industries than in manufacturing industries.
   4. A company with high output levels would employ fewer workers than a firm producing less output.

iii. **Market capitalisation**

   1. This measures the value of the firm on the stock exchange.
   2. It represents what people are prepared to pay for shares.
   3. It analyses the firm's present position and expected future position.
   4. The problem with this measure is that it can vary daily; share value can change based on perception.
   5. However, the measure cannot be used to measure size of firms generally, as most firms are not listed on the stock exchange.

iv. **Capital employed**

   1. This involves the total amount of capital invested in the firm.
   2. This will indicate the value of assets employed in the firm.
   3. This figure is sometimes expressed as a ratio of capital employed per worker.
   4. It is difficult to measure capital employed especially, since the value of assets may be determined differently.
   5. Capital employed may also depend on the other indicators.
   6. A firm, because of the nature of the output, may be labour intensive, have low output levels and use little capital.

v. **Total profits**

   1. Profit maximisation is the main objective of private sector firms
   2. Profitability is important to current and prospective shareholders
   3. Profits can be used to measure the size of firms
   4. However profits depend on more than just the size of the firm. They depend on:
      i. The level of efficiency of the firm
      ii. How motivated workers are
      iii. The effectiveness of management style
   5. Profits really determine how successful the firm is: not necessarily the size.

### b. Definition of size of business

i. The World Bank definition of size of firms is set out below.

| The World Bank definition of size of firms | | | |
|---|---|---|---|
| Size of firm | Number of employees | Sales turnover (US $) | Total assets (US $) |
| Micro | ≤ 10 | ≤ $100,000 | ≤ $100,000 |
| Small | ≤ 50 | ≤ $3 M | ≤ $3 M |
| Medium | ≤ 300 | ≤ $15 M | ≤ $15 M |

ii    Different definitions are used in different parts of the Caribbean to measure size of the firm. In Jamaica, the definition is as follows:

| Definition of size of firms used in Jamaica | | |
|---|---|---|
| Size of firm | Number of employees | Total sales turnover (J $) |
| Micro | ≤ 5 | ≤ $10 M |
| Small | 6 – 20 | > $10 M ≤ $50 M |
| Medium | 21 – 50 | >$50 M ≤ $150 M |

## c. The importance of small firms

1. Create employment: small firms are eventually labour intensive; this means they create employment especially for individuals that are unskilled or semi-skilled.
2. Opportunity for development of entrepreneurial talents:
   i.   Small firms provide an opportunity for the development of entrepreneurial talents.
   ii.  Individuals who like working for themselves may develop and convert their talents into a profitable enterprise.
3. In rural areas:
   i.   Small firms are found mainly in rural areas, where it would not be economical for large firms to operate and survive.
   ii.  They therefore satisfy the demand for goods and services in these rural areas
4. Good labour relations:
   i.   Small firms have good labour relations.
   ii.  Because they are small, there is better communication, workers are more motivated, and labour disputes are easily resolved.
   iii. There are no trade unions.
5. Improve the standard of living and quality of life: small firms therefore improve the standard of living and quality of life of workers.
6. Gross national product: small firms make a valuable contribution to the economy's gross national product
7. Provides inputs for larger firms:
   i.   Small firms provide inputs for larger firms
   ii.  They create that valuable backward link that allows production to be free of possible bottlenecks, e.g. small farmers that provide sorrel for the large manufacturing plant.
8. Potential to grow into larger business: small businesses have potential to grow into larger businesses, reap the benefits of economies of scale and be able to compete with other firms on the international market.

## Measuring growth of firms

1. Small firms can grow into larger firms through internal growth. Here the firms gain the benefits of economies of scale; e.g. marketing economies, risk-bearing economies, technical economies, financial economies, managerial economies, purchasing economies. This is seen through their growing markets, improvement in technology and even entering new markets.
2. The firm can also grow externally by integration, i.e., merging with other firms (where two or more firms are joined) or taking over other firms (where the shares of one firm are bought by another firm).
3. Growth can be classified in four ways:
   i.   Horizontal growth: this occurs where the firm takes over or merges with another firm in the same industry, at the same stage of production. (See below.)

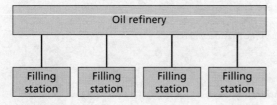

   ii.  Lateral growth: this occurs where firms take over another firm which does not provide its inputs or use its output. (See below.)

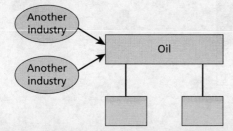

iii. Vertical growth: this is where the firm expands within the same industry with other firms, either through backward linkages or forward linkages. (See below.)

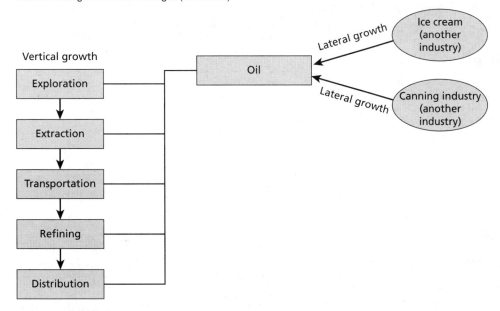

iv. Conglomerate: this occurs where the firm expands with other firms in a different industry that is not connected to the original line of the firm. (See below.)

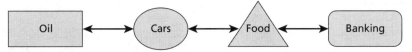

## d. Advantages and disadvantages of small firms vs large firms
### i. Small firms

| Advantages and disadvantages of small firms | |
| --- | --- |
| **Advantages** | **Disadvantages** |
| › Serve the local community in rural areas | › Face competition from larger firms |
| › Provide specialist services | › Cannot reap the benefits of economies of scale |
| › Provide inputs for larger firms | › Problems in obtaining capital |
| › Subcontracting: many small businesses survive by subcontracting to larger firms | › Poor management skills |
| › Can come together and purchase in bulk and gain the benefits of economies of scale | › Limited by government regulations, e.g. minimum wage |
| › Offer personal contact with customers | › For a very small firm, the cost maybe too high |
| › Being one's own 'boss'; to make all decisions | › If firm produces only one product, a change in demand may lead to a heavy financial burden |
| › Patents provide investors with exclusive rights to make a particular product for a specified number of years | › Loans are expensive to finance |
| › Copyright - offers protection for the printed material, e.g. a book | › Administration, accounting and filing forms, e.g. VAT, creates problems for small business |
| › Trademarks - they are symbols the firm uses to ensure protection of its products | |
| › Flexible: can adapt to customers need of working hours, designing products | |
| › Personal service: they fill the needs not met by large firms | |
| › Transport cost: they are located close to customers, therefore transport cost is low | |

ii. **Large firms**

| Advantages and disadvantages of large firms | |
|---|---|
| **Advantages** | **Disadvantages** |
| › Reap the benefits of economies of scale: these can be internal or external | › Do not offer personal service |
| › Internal economies of scale: these are the benefits a firm gains as it increases the size of its operations. These include:<br>o technical economies<br>o risk-bearing economies<br>o marketing economies<br>o financial economies | › May grow too large and experience diseconomies of scale |
| › External economies of scale: these are the benefits to the firm because of its location, or by virtue of being part of an industry. These include:<br>o Specialised workers<br>o Research and development<br>o Support from other firms in terms of training for workers<br>o Specialised services: banks , insurance, cleaning, catering become established to near Industrial areas | |

**Limitations on the growth of small firms**

1. **Size of market is limited by:**
   i. Small demand
   ii. Transport cost
   iii. Nature of product, e.g. perishable
2. **Available capital**
3. **Owner's personal preference**

 QUICK TEST

1. **Define the concept: 'small business'.**  [10 marks]
2. **Explain how a business can grow.**  [10 marks]
3. **State the importance of growth to a business.**  [10 marks]
4. **Why is it that some firms remain small?**  [10 marks]

# Major challenges and opportunities faced by small businesses

## Objectives

At the end of this section, you will know:

1. **The opportunities for small businesses**
2. **The challenges faced by small businesses**

### a. Identifying business opportunity

There are a number of areas that can create an opportunity for an entrepreneur to start a business:

1. Purchasing a franchise.
2. Identifying a gap in the market: the entrepreneur can identify a gap in the market (missing market) and produce a product that satisfies that demand.
3. Using existing skills: entrepreneurs are more likely to be successful if they use their existing skills to start their business.
4. Invention: entrepreneurs can start their business if they have invented a product. This allows the entrepreneurs to benefit from a niche market.

### b. Sourcing capital (finance)

1. One of the major problems facing the entrepreneur is the availability of finance. In Trinidad and Tobago, the government and non-government agencies offer assistance to entrepreneurs, but there is also a challenge to obtain the funding.
2. The main sources of funding for small businesses are as follows:
   i. Owner's savings: the challenge here is that this is usually insufficient to cover both fixed and variable costs
   ii. Friends and family: the challenge here is that if finance is provided, then they may want a part in the decision-making. The entrepreneur may not want this. In addition funds may still not be sufficient.
   iii. Banks: the banks will provide finance but at a high rate of interest. If the entrepreneur is late in repaying the loan, they will face additional charges. In addition, banks require collateral to guarantee repayment of the loan.
   iv. Venture capitalists: they will invest in a business if they believe their investment will bring returns. Usually small businesses cannot guarantee this.
   v. Government funding: The Trinidad and Tobago government provide funding for small businesses; however this is only available for specific purposes, e.g. NEDCO provides funding for machinery, not for construction of the building.
   vi. Business plan: funding would be denied if the business plan fails to convince the potential investor that the business is a viable one.

### c. Selection of types of business structure

A challenge facing small business is to select the type of business structure. Each type presents challenges and opportunities; therein lays the problem.

   i. Sole trader

| Sole trader | |
| --- | --- |
| **Opportunities** | **Challenges** |
| › Personal satisfaction of being one's own boss<br>› Freedom and flexibility in running own business<br>› Enjoy all the profits<br>› Few legal formalities in setting up the business; easy to form<br>› Owner has total control of the business<br>› Personal contact with workers so there is a better working environment<br>› Better able to cater to customers' needs because of personal contact with them<br>› Secrecy: no need to declare business accounts to anyone except the tax office | › Finance is limited<br>› It may not be possible to benefit from economies of scale<br>› Growth is restricted<br>› Specialisation is not possible<br>› Need to work long hours, leaving little time for anything else<br>› No continuity in the business if owner dies<br>› Unlimited liability |

ii. Partnerships

| Partnerships | |
|---|---|
| **Opportunities** | **Challenges** |
| › Relatively easy to form<br>› Profits are shared with a small number of partners<br>› The workload can be shared. It allows for a measure of specialisation among members<br>› A partner is usually flexible. Partners can enter and leave the partnership<br>› There is more free time for partners<br>› More capital can be raised than as a sole trader<br>› The partnership does not die on the death of a partner | › Resources are still limited<br>› All partners will lose if one partner makes a mistake<br>› Profits must be shared among partners<br>› There is the responsibility of disagreements among members<br>› Decisions may take longer |

iii. Private limited companies

| Private limited companies | |
|---|---|
| **Opportunities** | **Challenges** |
| › More capital is available<br>› More specialists can be brought into the business<br>› Privacy is retained<br>› Continuity is ensured. The death of a shareholder does not affect the company<br>› The company has a separate legal identity from those who own the company<br>› Shareholders have limited liability | › Capital is limited as members of the public cannot invest in the business<br>› Growth is slow<br>› Profits must be divided among the investors |

iv. Franchise

| Franchise | |
|---|---|
| **Opportunities** | **Challenges** |
| › The problems of starting a new business in terms of market research, etc., does not exist<br>› The franchise does not have to cover the cost of advertising<br>› Franchisee buys an already successful business<br>› The cost of research and development is borne by the franchisor | › The franchisee must share profits with the franchisor<br>› The cost of purchasing the franchise could be high<br>› The franchisee must obey the rules and regulations set out by the franchisor |

v. Cooperative

| Cooperative | |
|---|---|
| **Opportunities** | **Challenges** |
| › Employment is created within the organisation<br>› All members can benefit from bulk buying<br>› There is a guaranteed market for members<br>› Little or no advertising cost | › Management may lack the necessary expertise<br>› Cooperatives may find it difficult to attract skilled professionals<br>› Capital is limited |

## d. Determining the location

1. This is another challenge for the entrepreneur. The business needs to be located close to consumers. Such a location will normally be expensive for the entrepreneur, in terms of purchase or rent.
2. Operating the business from home is the most likely option; this decision, however, presents additional challenges as follows:
   i. It may be difficult to separate working life from private life
   ii. It may not be attractive enough for customers
   iii. It may be too far from the target market

## e. Globalisation and trade liberalisation

1. Globalisation: this is the trend for markets to become established worldwide. It is the trend towards free international trade and the free movement of capital between countries.
2. Benefits to small firms:
   i. New markets: small businesses in Trinidad and Tobago can do their market research and cater for the international markets, e.g. markets in South America.
   ii. Cheaper inputs: small firms are now able to fund cheaper sources of new materials.

   iii.  Competition: small firms are now forced to become more efficient if they are to survive in the face of competition.

   iv.  Learning by doing: small firms are able to learn the production process and marketing strategies of larger firms and in the long run to compete with them for market share.

3.  Challenges to small firms

   i.  Competition: small businesses, e.g. the local garment producer in Trinidad and Tobago, will find it difficult to compete with the more established brand-named items that are imported.

   ii.  Contraction of the domestic industry: domestic producers would reallocate resources out of the garment industry

## f. E-Commerce

1.  Opportunities to small firms

   i.  Niche market: small business may be able to identify a niche in the international markets for their products.

   ii.  Inputs: small businesses may be able to obtain inputs at a lower price. This reduces their cost of production and selling price.

   iii.  Economies of scale: small businesses may be able to experience some measure of economies of scale as demand for their output increases.

2.  Challenges to small firms

   i.  Contraction of domestic manufacturing industry: small businesses, e.g. the garment industry in Trinidad and Tobago, are experiencing a fall in demand for their output as local domestic consumers now purchase items online at a cheaper cost.

   ii.  Retail outlets: small businesses that sell garments that were previously imported now find the demand for their products has fallen, as consumers buy directly from suppliers.

## g. Intellectual property

1.  This is a legal term that refers to the creations of the mind. For example, literature, music, etc.

2.  It includes:

   i.  Patents: this offers protection to investors. It gives them exclusive rights to manufacture a given product.

   ii.  Copyright: this applies to all printed materials, e.g. books. It offers protection to workers that their work will not be copied without their permission.

   iii.  Trademarks: these may be a symbol used by a producer to distinguish its product from its rival product.

3.  There are therefore opportunities for small business to be protected from larger firms.

 QUICK TEST

1.  **List and discuss the major challenges facing small business in your country.**    **[15 marks]**

2.  **List and discuss the opportunities that exist for small business in your country.**    **[15 marks]**

# Types and nature of assistance available to small firms

## Objectives

At the end of this section, you will know:

1. **How the following agencies assist small businesses:**
   a. Government agencies
   b. Non-governmental agencies
   c. Financial institutions
2. **The types of assistance offered to small businesses.**

## Introduction

Small businesses and the increase in entrepreneurial talent are vital for the economic transformation of Caribbean economies.

To achieve this, government must work in conjunction with non-governmental agencies and financial institutions to create the necessary climate to foster growth of small businesses.

### a. Agencies that assist small businesses in Trinidad and Tobago

1. Governmental agencies Aid Program
2. Non-governmental agencies
3. Financial Institutions

#### i. Government agencies in Trinidad and Tobago

1. The National Enterprise Development Company (NEDCO)
   i. It has as its slogan: 'We support. You succeed.'
   ii. NEDCO offers financial support and advice for small and micro-enterprises. NEDCO also provides funding to start a business or additional funding, where needed, for an existing business. It provides finding for individuals who must have the following requirements:
      a. A registered business
      b. A business plan
      c. A profit and loss statement if it is an existing business
      d. Aged over 18 years and be a citizen of Trinidad and Tobago.
2. The Ministry of Community Development
   i. The Ministry of Community Development provide training for women to enable them to acquire marketable skills, e.g. cake decorating, dress-making, hairdressing and beauty culture
   ii. The Ministry also organises courses to assist those acquiring the necessary skills to help them to establish their own business.
3. Micro Enterprise Loan Facility
   Financial assistance is given to individuals, as well as assistance in the preparation of a business plan.
4. The Micro Enterprise Training Grant
   i. This grant is made available for anyone who requires funding for a new business venture or to develop their own skills.
   ii. Personnel from the Ministry of Social Development work closely with those receiving aid to ensure the success of the program.
5. The Agricultural Development Bank
   › The objective is to aid the development and growth of the fishing, forestry and agricultural industries.
   › The bank provides assistance in the form of loans, business advice, business management training technical skills.
6. The Capital Incentive Programmes
   This program was introduced to assist small businesses to obtain finance. The program offers tax credit to investors who qualify.

#### ii. Non-governmental agencies

Non-governmental agencies are organisations in the private sector that give assistance to small businesses.

1. The Business Development Company
   i. The Business Development Company was established by the Government of Trinidad and Tobago in 2002. It is now a limited company.
   ii. It offers a loan guarantee program to assist small businesses in obtaining loans from lending agencies. It also works in conjunction with the Ministry of Trade and Industry to administer the approval of the small company status scheme.
   iii. A business registered with the scheme would pay less corporation taxes on profits, but to be registered the business must:
      a. be locally owned and controlled

    b. have at least five permanent employees

    c. make use of local raw material

2. Youth Business of Trinidad and Tobago

    i. Youth Business of Trinidad and Tobago began operating in 2000.

    ii. It provides micro credit to young entrepreneurs, in addition to training and support.

3. Cooperative Credit Union League of Trinidad and Tobago

    Cooperative Credit Union League of Trinidad and Tobago provides training to credit union members

4. Credit Unions

    Credit Unions give loans to their members who want to establish a small business. Some also provide necessary training and organise craft markets.

5. Women World Banking of Trinidad and Tobago

    i. Women World Banking of Trinidad and Tobago's main objective is to promote women as entrepreneurs.

    ii. It provides loans to women entrepreneurs.

    iii. It provides training.

    iv. It provides advisory services.

    v. It guarantees that women may borrow from other lending institutions.

6. Fund-Aid Trinidad and Tobago Development Foundation Limited

    i. Fund-aided Trinidad and Tobago Development Foundation Limited provides loans to entrepreneurs if they can get three persons to guarantee the loan.

    ii. It conducts training and workshops.

    iii. It provides whatever technical advice is needed.

    iv. It provides whatever accounting service is needed.

7. Financial Institutions in Trinidad and Tobago

    Financial institutions in Trinidad and Tobago include banks and credit unions, which provide small business loans and other financial banking services, e.g. insurance, business accounts, mortgage advice and support. Examples include: Republic Bank, First Citizens Bank, and Teachers Credit Union.

## b. Types of assistance offered to small businesses

### i. Financial assistance

One of the major problems facing small businesses is obtaining the necessary finance. Financial assistance for small businesses can take the form of:

› Loan guarantees: this enables the firm to purchase assets necessary for production.

› Venture capital: this is capital that private investors put into the business.

› Working capital finance: this is money needed to finance the daily expenses of the business.

› Debt factoring: this allows the business to improve its cash flow.

### ii. Technical assistance

› This is needed to ensure the success of the business

› The assistance will include:

    o Information in relation to stock holding

    o Information on how to set up and use machinery

    o Information on how to control pollution

    o Specialist advice can be obtained from organisations (e.g. hairdressers associations, association of craft entrepreneurs, the pharmacy associations)

    o There are a number of educational institutions in Trinidad & Tobago, that provide training in the technical field e.g. University of the West Indies

### iii. Education & training

› Government agencies, non-governmental agencies and financial institutions provide education and training facilities for entrepreneurs

› Training in:

    o marketing and promoting the business

    o legal issues, e.g. employment laws

    o keeping accurate financial records

    o The University of the West Indies offer degree programs in business management

    o NEDCO has established its Entrepreneurial Training Institute and Incubation Centre (ETHC); this provides specialised knowledge and advisory service in all areas of entrepreneurship, e.g. legal issues, tax and finance

 QUICK TEST

1. **Why is it necessary for small firms to seek assistance?** [10 marks]

2. **State the types of assistance the government offers to small firms.** [10 marks]

3. **Name the agencies that offer assistance to small firms.** [6 marks]

# Preparation of a business plan for a small business

## Objectives

At the end of this section, you will know:

1. **What a business plan is.**
2. **The value of a business plan to a small business.**
3. **The essential features of a business plan.**

### a. Definition of a business plan

1. A business plan gives a complete description of a business.
2. It tells what the business plan is to do.
3. How the business plan is to do it.
4. It is a formal statement of the business goals, the reason they are believed to be attainable and the plans for reaching the goals.
5. It represents all aspects of the business planning process and it shows the interrelationship among the different departments of the business, e.g. marketing, finance, production, human relations, as well as a legal plan.

### Value of the business plan

1. Owners of small businesses will be required to present a business plan when they are seeking financial assistance from any lending institution.
2. It is useful for helping the entrepreneur to think through their ideas before actually beginning the business.
3. The act of planning helps to clarify the objectives and strategies of the business in the mind of the entrepreneur.
4. It is a working document that helps the entrepreneur to look at the current operations of the business and to plan for the future of the business.

### Sections of a business plan

A business plan can be divided into the following sections:

> Executive summary
> Business description
> Business environment analysis
> Industry background
> Competitor analysis
> Market analysis
> Marketing plan
> Operations plan
> Managerial summary
> Financial plan

### b. Executive summary

> It gives a clear picture of the main points of the business plan
> The amount of external finance needed
> The objectives of the business
> The product being produced
> Forms of ownership, e.g. sole trader, partnership, etc.
> The main strength of the business
> It should be written in order to persuade potential investors to invest money in the business

### c. Business description:

i. Legal establishment
ii. Start-up plans
> Is it a sole trader or partnership company?
> State the name of the business
> Description of the product or service
> Give an overview of start-up plan

### d. Business environment analysis:

i. Target market
ii. Customer needs
iii. Location
> What segment of the market is the firm catering for?
> What the customer needs? E.g. high-quality goods at a low price.
> Why is the location suitable?

**e. Industry background:**

   i. Give a concise account of the background to the industry

   ii. How big is the market?

**f. Competitor analysis:**

   › Who are the firm's competitors?

   › Name the competitors

   › Give a broad account about the firm's target market; this should include age, gender and income of persons.

**g. Market analysis:**

   i. Customer needs

   ii. Where are they

   iii. How to reach them

      › Based on market research, the following information will be obtained:

        o The size of the market

        o Market trends identified

        o Description of target customer

        o Share of market intended to gain

        o Any anticipated market threats

        o Degree of competition

        o How to gain customer loyalty

        o Customer awareness in the form of advertising and sales promotion

        o Where the product will be sold

**h. Market plan:**

   i. Pricing strategy

   ii. Promotion strategy

   iii. Distribution strategy

      › Give, in detail, marketing strategies to be followed

      › This will include:

        o Pricing policy to be used

        o Advertising and other forms of promotion

        o Selling and distribution of product

        o Launching the product

        o Developing the product

**i. Operations plan:**

   i. Cost of production

   ii. Machinery

      › This section deals with the cost of the goods or services

      › Location of production facility

      › Techniques and capital equipment needed for production

**j. Managerial summary:**

   i. Management personnel

   ii. Staffing

      › It deals with management personnel; number of employees

      › Who will manage the business?

      › What are their qualifications? (skills/ training)

**k. Financial plan:**

   i. Profit & Loss Account

   ii. Cash Flows

   iii. Break-even analysis

   iv. Source of funds

   v. Business ratios

   vi. Assumptions

      › This plan will depend upon whether the firm is an existing business or start-up.

      › If it is an existing business, it must include the balance sheet, profit & loss accounts, cash statements.

      › For start-up and existing businesses include:

        o Budget for the main functional areas

        o Cash flow forecasts

        o Costing and break-even analysis

        o Budgeted profit and loss accounts

        o Budgeted balance sheet

        o Total borrowing requirements

        o Total working capital requirements

        o Proposal of payment

- o Business ratios
- o Source of funds
> What are the main types of finance required?
> Who will provide them?
> Give a calculation of the capital needed to break even.
> What will the profit and loss account look like at the end of the first year?
> Business ratios formulae: (*See discussion of ratios in Unit 1 Module 3 – Business Finance & Accounting*).

- o **Liquidity ratios:**
  - (i) The current ratio:

$$\text{Current ratio} = \frac{\text{Current assets}}{\text{Current liabilities}}$$

  - (ii) Acid test (or quick) ratio:

$$\text{Acid test (quick) ratio} = \frac{\text{(cash + debtors) or (current assets – stock)}}{\text{Current liabilities}}$$

- o **Profitability ratios:**
  - (i) Gross profit margin:

$$\text{Gross profit margin} = \frac{\text{Gross profit} \times 100}{\text{Sales}}$$

  - (ii) Gross profit mark-up:

$$\text{Gross profit mark-up} = \frac{\text{Gross profit} \times 100}{\text{Cost of Sales}}$$

  - (iii) Return on capital employed (ROCE):

$$\text{ROCE} = \frac{\text{Net profit before interest and tax} \times 100}{\text{Total capital employed}}$$

  - (iv) Net profit margin:

$$\text{Net profit margin} = \frac{\text{Net profit (earnings before interest and tax)} \times 100}{\text{Sales revenue}}$$

- o **Efficiency/Activity ratios:**
  - (i) Stock turnover ratio:

$$\text{Stock turnover} = \frac{\text{Cost of sales for period}}{\text{Average stock}}$$

$$\text{Where average stock} = \frac{\text{(Opening stock + closing stock)}}{2}$$

  - (ii) Average trade debtor collection period or Debtor days:

$$\text{Debt collection} = \frac{\text{Average trade debtors} \times 365 \text{ period}}{\text{Total credit sales}}$$

  - (iii) Average trade creditor payment period or Creditor days:

$$\text{Credit payment} = \frac{\text{Average trade creditors} \times 365 \text{ period}}{\text{Total credit purchases}}$$

- o **Gearing ratio**

$$\text{Gearing ratio} = \frac{\text{Debt}}{\text{Capital employed}} \times 100$$

Where,
Debt = Long term debts
Capital employed = Fixed assets + current assets – current liabilities

- o **Investors/Shareholder ratios**
  - (i) Dividend yield:

$$\text{Dividend yield} = \frac{\text{Declared dividend per share}}{\text{Market share price}} \times 100$$

  - (ii) Earnings per share (EPS):

$$\text{EPS} = \frac{\text{Profits available for ordinary shareholders}}{\text{Number of shares}}$$

**Note:**
1. There is no fixed content for a business plan.
2. The content and format of the business plan is determined by the goals to be achieved.
3. A business plan for a non-profit organisation may show goals and objectives in relation to the organisation's mission/purpose.
4. The business plan for a bank loan will be structured to show the firm's ability to repay the loan.
5. A good business plan does not guarantee success but can reduce the risk of failure.
6. There is a difference between a forecast and plan; a forecast is a prediction of events over which, one has no control, whereas a plan is a statement of action to be taken.

 QUICK TEST

1. State the reasons for a business to have a business plan. **[10 marks]**
2. Why is it necessary to update a business plan? **[10 marks]**
3. List the items that should be included in a business plan. **[10 marks]**

## Key concepts

**Copyright:** this is protection granted by law to authors or written work or those who have recorded materials; these include books, films or music.

**External economies of scale:** these are the benefits to the firm because of its location or being part of an industry. These include:

› **Specialised workers**
› **Research and development**
› **Support from other firms in terms of training for workers**
› **Specialised services: banks, insurance, cleaning, catering become established to near industrial areas.**

**Globalisation:** this is the trend for markets to become established worldwide. It is the trend towards free international trade and the free movement of capital between countries.

**Internal economies of scale:** these are the benefits a firm gains as it increases the size of its operations. These include:

› **Technical economies**
› **Risk-bearing economies**
› **Marketing economies**
› **Financial economies**

**Target market:** it is that part of the market to which a firm aims to sell its products.

## Questions

1. State the importance of a business plan to:
   a. The owners of the business. **[8 marks]**
   b. Those who supply inputs for the business. **[8 marks]**
   c. Those who provide finance for the business. **[8 marks]**
2. State and explain the disadvantages that small firms face when compared to large firms. **[15 marks]**
3. State and explain the advantages of small firms when compared to large firms. **[15 marks]**
4. Do you think that the government of your country should assist small businesses? If No, give reasons for your answer.
5. a. List the financial institutions that assist small businesses in your country.
   b. State the terms and conditions under which they do. **[25 marks]**
6. State and explain the opportunities present in your country for the survival and growth of small businesses. **[25 marks]**
7. Discuss the contributions of small businesses to the development of your country. **[25 marks]**

## MULTIPLE CHOICE QUESTIONS

**1.** The following are characteristics of a successful entrepreneur except:
a. A risk-taker
b. Goal-oriented
c. Persistent optimistic
d. Not sociable

**2.** Which of the following is the best definition of the entrepreneur?
a. Someone who has the ability to work hard
b. Someone who invents a new product
c. Someone who has a vast amount of business ideas
d. Someone who takes the financial risk of starting a new business

**3.** The following are the criteria for measuring the size of a firm:
I. The level of output
II. The size of the labour force
III. The amount of the capital employed
IV. The number of products the firm produces
a. I, II
b. I, II, III
c. III, IV
d. II, IV

**4.** Management can foster the spirit of entrepreneurship by:
a. Training workers to be entrepreneurs
b. Management should be more autocratic
c. Leaving workers to develop their own ideas
d. Motivating workers so that they are comfortable to voice their ideas while reminding them that not all of their ideas could be undertaken by the firm

**5.** Small firms enjoy the following advantages over large firms:
I. They provide specialist services
II. They can come together and purchase in bulk and reap the benefits of economies of scale
III. They are flexible and can adapt to customer needs
IV. Low transport cost as they are located close to customers
a. I, II
b. I, IV
c. I, II, III
d. I, II, III, IV

**6.** The size of the market is limited by:
I. Small demand
II. Transport cost
III. The nature of the product
IV. The owners personal preference
a. I, II
b. I, IV
c. I, III
d. I, II, III, IV

**7.** A small business might find it difficult to expand because:
I. They lack sufficient finance
II. They lack technical and managerial skills
III. The government does not provide sufficient support
IV. There is an inadequate supply of labour
a. I, II
b. II, III, IV
c. II, III
d. I, II, III, IV

**8.** Which of the following are the challenges faced by a private limited company?
I. Capital is limited
II. Growth is slow
III. Profits must be divided among investors
IV. Their accounts must be made public
a. I, II
b. I, IV
c. I, II, III
d. I, II, III, IV

**9.** Ratios must be used with caution because:
a. They cannot be interpreted correctly
b. Ratios based on published accounts may not be valid today
c. They do not relate to all aspects of the firm
d. They are difficult to calculate

**10.** The business plan is a statement that relates to the business in terms of:
I. The current situation if the business is established
II. The objectives of the business
III. How it will achieve its objectives
IV. The viability of the proposal
a. I, III
b. I, II
c. I
d. I, II, III, IV

**11.** A business plan is a document that:
I. Gives a complete description of the business
II. Tells what the business plans to do
III. Outlines the business goals and the plans for reaching them
IV. Shows the inter-relationship among the different departments
a. I, II
b. I, III, IV
c. I, II, IV
d. I, II, III, IV

**12.** It is necessary to re-visit the business plan periodically because:
a. The firm has the time to do so
b. Of changes in the external environment
c. The bank requires this
d. The shareholders believe this is necessary

13. A conglomerate occurs where:
    a. A firm expands with another firm in a different industry that is not connected to the original line of the firm
    b. A firm takes over another firm
    c. Workers from one firm can be transferred to another firm
    d. The firm reaps the benefits of economies of scale

14. Firms can grow externally:
    a. By integration
    b. By reaping the benefits of economies of scale
    c. By having large amounts of retained profits
    d. By moving to a new location

15. E-commerce provides the following opportunities for small firms:
    a. A niche market
    b. Linkages with other firms
    c. Gain financial aid from the government
    d. Be able to access loans from the banks

16. Globalisation provides the following advantages for small firms:
    I. New markets
    II. Learning by doing
    III. Cheaper inputs
    IV. Transfer of technology

    a. I, IV
    b. I, II, III
    c. I, III, IV
    d. I, II, III, IV

# ANSWERS FOR MULTIPLE CHOICE QUESTIONS

## UNIT 1: MANAGEMENT PRINCIPLES AND PROCESSES

### Module 1: Business and its Environment

| | | | |
|---|---|---|---|
| 1. | c | 10. | d |
| 2. | d | 11. | c |
| 3. | a | 12. | b |
| 4. | c | 13. | d |
| 5. | a | 14. | d |
| 6. | d | 15. | a |
| 7. | b | 16. | b |
| 8. | a | 17. | d |
| 9. | b | 18. | b |

### Module 2: The Management of People

| | | | |
|---|---|---|---|
| 1. | b | 10. | d |
| 2. | a | 11. | a |
| 3. | b | 12. | a |
| 4. | b | 13. | b |
| 5. | b | 14. | a |
| 6. | c | 15. | c |
| 7. | c | 16. | a |
| 8. | b | 17. | c |
| 9. | a | 18. | c |

### Module 3: Business Finance & Accounting

| | | | |
|---|---|---|---|
| 1. | c | 8. | c |
| 2. | b | 9. | b |
| 3. | a | 10. | b |
| 4. | a | 11. | c |
| 5. | c | 12. | c |
| 6. | a | 13. | d |
| 7. | a | 14. | c |

## UNIT 2: APPLICATIONS IN MANAGEMENT

### Module 1: Productions and Operations Management

| | | | |
|---|---|---|---|
| 1. | d | 10. | b |
| 2. | c | 11. | a |
| 3. | d | 12. | a |
| 4. | c | 13. | d |
| 5. | d | 14. | b |
| 6. | d | 15. | c |
| 7. | d | 16. | d |
| 8. | a | 17. | c |
| 9. | a | 18. | a |

### Module 2: Fundamentals of Marketing

| | | | |
|---|---|---|---|
| 1. | d | 11. | b |
| 2. | c | 12. | a |
| 3. | d | 13. | d |
| 4. | b | 14. | b |
| 5. | b | 15. | c |
| 6. | c | 16. | c |
| 7. | a | 17. | d |
| 8. | c | 18. | d |
| 9. | b | 19. | d |
| 10. | d | 20. | b |

### Module 3: Small Business Management

| | | | |
|---|---|---|---|
| 1. | d | 11. | d |
| 2. | d | 12. | b |
| 3. | b | 13. | a |
| 4. | d | 14. | a |
| 5. | d | 15. | a |
| 6. | d | 16. | b |
| 7. | a | | |
| 8. | c | | |
| 9. | b | | |
| 10. | d | | |

# Index